READY, SET, GO!®

NJ ASK
Language Arts Literacy
Grade 3

Staff of Research & Education Association
Piscataway, New Jersey

Research & Education Association
Visit our website at
www.rea.com

The Performance Standards in this book were created and implemented by the New Jersey State Department of Education. For further information, visit the Department of Education website at *www.state.nj.us/njded/cccs.*

Research & Education Association
61 Ethel Road West
Piscataway, New Jersey 08854
E-mail: info@rea.com

Ready, Set, Go!®
New Jersey ASK
Language Arts Literacy
Grade 3

Printed in the United States of America

Library of Congress Control Number 2009940386

ISBN-13: 978-0-7386-0797-9
ISBN-10: 0-7386-0797-5

Contents

Section 1: Reading

Section 2: Writing

About Research & Education Association

Founded in 1959, Research & Education Association (REA) is dedicated to publishing the finest and most effective educational materials—including software, study guides, and test preps—for students in elementary school, middle school, high school, college, graduate school, and beyond.

Today REA's wide-ranging catalog is a leading resource for teachers, students, and professionals.

We invite you to visit us at *www.rea.com* to find out how "REA is making the world smarter."

Acknowledgments

We would like to thank REA's Larry B. Kling, Vice President, Editorial, for supervising development; Pam Weston, Vice President, Publishing, for setting the quality standards for production integrity and managing the publication to completion; Alice Leonard, Senior Editor, for project management, editorial guidance, and preflight editorial review of new edition; Diane Goldschmidt, Senior Editor, for post-production quality assurance; Rachel DiMatteo, Graphic Artist, for her design contributions; and Christine Saul, Senior Graphic Artist, for cover design.

We also gratefully acknowledge the writers, educators, and editors of REA and Northeast Editing for content development, editorial guidance, and final review. Thanks to Andrea Gianchiglia for her wonderful illustrations, to Matrix Publishing for page design, and to Kathy Caratozzolo of Caragraphics for typesetting the new edition.

A special thank you to Lisa Fontana, third grade teacher, in Crescent School of the Waldwick School District, NJ, for her advice and input to this edition.

Introduction

Welcome to an Educational Adventure

The New Jersey Assessment of Skills and Knowledge, or NJ ASK, is a special milestone, as it represents the first time that New Jersey's public school students are presented with a state-mandated standardized test. Indeed, the ASK is the Garden State's answer to the federal No Child Left Behind Act, which requires that states use standards-based testing to ensure that students are picking up the skills and knowledge necessary for academic success.

We at REA believe that a friendly, hands-on introduction and preparation for the test are keys to creating a successful testing experience. REA's NJ ASK books offer these key features:

✓ Clearly identified book activities

✓ Contextual illustrations

✓ Easy-to-follow lessons

✓ Step-by-step examples

✓ Tips for solving problems tailored for the proper grade level

✓ Exercises to sharpen skills

✓ Real practice

Below is helpful information for students, parents, and teachers concerning the NJ ASK and test taking in general. Organized practice is itself a prime skill for young students to master, because it will help set the tone for success long into the future as their educational adventure continues. It is REA's sincere hope that this book—by providing relevant, standards-based practice—can become an integral part of that adventure.

What is the NJ ASK?

The New Jersey Assessment of Skills and Knowledge is a standards-based assessment used in New Jersey's public schools. Performance on the NJ ASK test equates not with the grades students receive for teacher-assigned work but rather with proficiency measures pegged to how well students are acquiring the knowledge and skills outlined in the state's Core Curriculum Content Standards. Those proficiency measures fall into three broad categories, or bands: "partially proficient," "proficient," and "advanced proficient."

When is the NJ ASK given?

The test is administered in early spring. Grade 3 students take the NJ ASK Language Arts Literacy on two days and the Mathematics test on the next two days, the final morning in Mathematics. Grade 4 students take the test on five mornings, the first two in Language Arts Literacy, the next two days in Mathematics, and the last in Science. Each day's test spans 54 to 90 minutes, not including time to distribute materials, read directions, and take breaks.

What is the format of the NJ ASK?

The NJ ASK has two types of questions: multiple choice and open ended. With multiple choice, students are asked to choose the one correct answer out of the four choices provided. With open-ended questions, children answer with written responses in their own words. Each test section is timed, and students may not proceed to the next section until time for the current section has expired. If students have not finished a section when time runs out, they must stop and put down their pencils. There are clear directions throughout the test.

Understanding the NJ ASK and This Book

Students:

This book was specially written and designed to make test practice easy and fruitful for you. Our practice tests are very much like the actual NJ ASK tests, and our review is filled with illustrations, drills, exercises, and practice questions to help you become familiar with the testing environment and to retain information about key topics.

Parents:

The NJ ASK and other state assessment tests are designed to give the school information about how well children are achieving in the areas required by New Jersey's Core Curriculum Content Standards, which describe what students should know at the end of certain grades. This book will help your child review and prepare effectively and positively for the NJ ASK in Language Arts Literacy.

Teachers:

As their teacher, you introduce your students to the test-taking environment and the demands of the NJ ASK tests. You can use our authoritative book in your classroom for planned, guided instruction and practice testing. Effective preparation means better test scores!

Updates to the NJASK:

The test information in this book is taken directly from the *2009 Score Interpretation Manual Grades 3–8* of October 2009.

Where can I obtain more information about the NJ ASK?

For more information about the NJ ASK, contact the state Department of Education or Measurement, Inc,:

www.state.nj.us/education/assessement

www.measinc.com/njask

Office of Evaluation and Assessment
Telephone: 609-292-4469
Mailing address:
New Jersey Department of Education
PO Box 500
Trenton, NJ 08625-05000

For more information on the National Assessment of Educational Process:
(NAEP) Writing Frameworks: *http://nagb.org/publications/frameworks.htm*

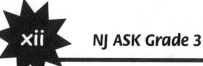

Test Accommodations and Special Situations

Every effort is made to provide a level playing field for students with disabilities who are taking the NJ ASK. Most students with educational disabilities and most students whose English language skills are limited take the standard NJ ASK. Students with disabilities will be working toward achieving the standards at whatever level is appropriate for them. Supports such as large-print type are available for students who have a current Individualized Education Program (IEP) or who have plans required under Section 504 or who use these supports and accommodations during other classroom testing.

If the IEP team decides that a student will not take the NJ ASK in Language Arts Literacy, Mathematics, and/or Science, the child will take the Alternate Proficiency Assessment (APA).

Tips for Test Taking

- **Do your homework.** From the first assignment of the year, organize the day so there is always time to study and keep up with homework.

- **Communicate.** If there are any questions, doubts, or concerns about anything relating to school, study, or tests, speak up. This goes for teachers and parents, as well as students.

- **Get some rest.** Getting a good night's sleep the night before the test is essential to waking up sharp and focused.

- **Eat right.** Having a good breakfast—nothing very heavy—the morning of the test is what the body and mind need. Comfortable clothes, plenty of time to get to school, and the confidence of having prepared properly are all any student needs.

- **Test smart.** Read the questions carefully. Make sure answers are written correctly in the proper place on the answer sheet. Don't rush, and don't go too slow. If there is time, go back and check questions that you weren't sure about.

Format of the NJ ASK Language Arts Literacy Test

The reading portion of the test contains three passages with a total of 18 multiple-choice questions. The writing portion requires students to write two essays: one in response to an expository prompt that introduces a topic and the other in response to an expository prompt that begins with a poem that introduces a topic. The table below outlines the assessment clusters, the types of writing tasks, and the amount of time students have to work on the questions on the reading and writing portions.

Assessment Cluster	Task	Time
1. Writing: speculate prompt	Story	30 minutes
2. Reading: narrative	6 MC,* 1 OE*	50 minutes
3. Listening/Reading: poem	6 MC,* 1 OE*	30 minutes
4. Writing: expository prompt	Composition	30 minutes
5. Reading: everyday text	6 MC, 1 OE	25 minutes

*MC = "multiple choice"; OE = "open-ended."

In 2009, a third reading passage was added to the test, along with an additional 6 MC and 1 OE. According to the NJDOE, the placement of this passage will vary. We have placed one additional reading passage in Day 1 of Practice Test 1, and another in Day 2 of Practice Test 2. The total for each test is now 3 passages with a total of 18 MC questions and 3 OE questions.

For the NJ ASK, **narrative reading** text is defined as literature written primarily to tell a story. These passages have a conflict and address common aspects of human nature. For Grade 3, narrative passages are selected from previously published literature of approximately 500 and 1,000 words. Narrative passages chosen for the NJ ASK contain the following elements:

- Significant themes that are age appropriate and grade-level appropriate

- A clearly identifiable problem/conflict and resolution

- A well-organized plot with clearly developed and meaningful events

- Well-developed characters

- Settings integral to the plot

- Literary elements, such as imagery and foreshadowing

- A range of vocabulary for which adequate context is provided

On the NJ ASK, **informational reading** or everyday text is defined as text that people encounter in their daily lives. It is written and designed to convey information about a topic and/or to show how to do something. Texts of varying formats are selected and/or adapted from previously published sources, such as magazines, newspapers, how-to books, and hands-on activity kits and workbooks. Everyday texts for Grade 3 range in length from approximately 400 to 900 words. The text has a strong central idea or purpose and contains the following elements:

- Engaging topics that are age appropriate and grade-level appropriate

- A clear, positive focus

- A clearly developed explanation of ideas, activities, or action

- A clearly developed sequence of ideas, activities, or actions

- Performable activities or actions

- Vivid and clear illustrations

- A range of vocabulary for which adequate context is provided

The writing prompts present topics that allow students to draw on material in the assessment, as well as from their own prior knowledge, to establish a context for their writing. In one task, students read a prompt and use their understanding of the prompt to develop a story. In a second task, students might listen to a poem read by the examiner as they read the poem silently. They respond to a written prompt that extends an idea introduced by the poem.

Each writing task provides space for students to plan their ideas. Students are encouraged to use that space to organize their ideas using a prewriting strategy (e.g., making a web, a list, or some other sort of graphic organizer) of their own choosing. The instructions direct students to write their own story or composition on the lined pages provided. This version of their writing is considered a first draft.

Each type of writing task is administered in a consistent format and in a constant time segment of 30 minutes. Students are instructed to use the first few minutes to develop ideas for their writing and to use the last few minutes to review and revise what they have written.

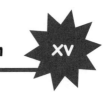

Scoring the Test

On the reading portion of the Grade 3 NJ ASK, each multiple-choice question is worth 1 point. Open-ended questions are scored holistically on a 0- to 4-point scale. The highest score a student can achieve on the reading portion of the test is 20 points.

Rubric for Scoring Open-Ended Questions

Points	Criteria
4	A 4-point response clearly demonstrates understanding of the task, fulfills all requirements, and provides a clear and focused explanation/opinion that links to or extends aspects of the text.
3	A 3-point response demonstrates an understanding of the task, addresses all requirements, and provides some explanation/opinion using situations or ideas from the text as support.
2	A 2-point response may address all of the requirements, but it demonstrates a partial understanding of the task and uses text incorrectly or with limited success, resulting in an inconsistent or flawed explanation.
1	A 1-point response demonstrates minimal understanding of the task, does not address part of the requirements, and provides only a vague reference to or no use of the text.
0	A 0-point response is irrelevant or off-topic.

Writing tasks are scored through use of a holistic scoring rubric developed specifically to focus on essential features of good writing and to assess students' performance in composing written language. Each writing sample is scored on a 1- to 5-point scale, which is a modified version of New Jersey's Registered Holistic Scoring Rubric.

*Standards with a *W* (for "working with text") focus on ideas and information that are presented in the text and available either literally or by extrapolation. Standards with an *A* (for "analyzing/ critiquing text") focus on students' analysis of what they have read.

NJ ASK Language Arts Literacy Standards

W1* Recognition of a Central Idea or Theme   A central idea or theme is a statement that is broad enough to cover the entire scope of the reading passage. The central idea or theme may be stated or implied, but clues to it are found in the ideas that tend to recur in the text. Examples of a central idea or theme statement include the following:

>   **Imagination helps us to solve problems.**
>   **Ordinary objects can be used to create unusual art.**

W2   Recognition of Supporting Details   These questions focus on meaningful details that contribute to the development of a character or the plot or that develop ideas and information that are essential to the central idea of a text.

W3   Extrapolation of Information   These questions focus on ideas and information that are implied by, but are not explicit in, the text. For example, students may be asked to draw from cues provided in the text in order to identify how a character feels.

W4   Paraphrasing, Vocabulary   These questions focus on the meaning of words used in the text and elicit students' use of effective reading strategies to determine the meaning of the words. Targeted vocabulary always occurs within a semantic and syntactic context that students should draw on to respond to the question.

W5   Recognition of Text Organization   Text organization encompasses the patterns of organization that characterize the respective genres. For the narratives, questions focus on setting, character, and plot, as well as on any distinctive pattern, such as repetition, within the story. For everyday texts, questions address structural features, such as section topics, charts, and illustrations, in addition to patterns of organization within the text (such as sequence, comparison-contrast, or cause and effect).

W6   Recognition of a Purpose for Reading   These questions, which focus on the reader's purpose, address reasons for reading a particular text. A story, for example, may convey specific information about a species of animal or a culture, although that may not be the primary purpose of the text.

A1   Questioning, Clarifying, Predicting   These questions draw on students' use of reading strategies to construct meaning. The questions introduce a focus and a context for responding (e.g., asking a question of the author or a character) and ask students to select and analyze ideas and information from the text to develop a response. Given the nature of this task, these questions are almost always open-ended items.

A2   Prediction of Tentative Meaning   These questions focus on statements within the text that introduce some ambiguity: either the ideas are not fully explained or the statement uses language that can be read in two or more ways. For these questions, students use their knowledge of language and of the context within the reading passage to analyze the meaning of a particular statement.

A3   Forming of Opinions   These questions elicit students' responses to aspects of the text. The questions introduce a focus (e.g., whether the main character would make a good friend) and ask students to select and analyze ideas and information from the text to develop a response. Given the nature of this task, these questions are always open-ended items.

A4   Making Judgments, Drawing Conclusions   These questions ask students to draw conclusions based on knowledge they have garnered from the ideas and information within the text. For example, students might be asked to analyze how the setting (e.g., the season of the year) affects the sequence of events within a story or to analyze the effect of skipping a step in a certain procedure.

A5   Literary Elements and Textual Conventions   These questions focus on devices used by the author. Students might be asked to analyze what a specific metaphor conveys about a character in the story, or why an author uses italics for certain words.

NJ ASK Language Arts Literacy Standards*

W1	Recognition of a Central Idea or Theme	page 3
W2	Recognition of Supporting Details	page 3
W3	Extrapolation of Information	page 31
W4	Paraphrasing, Vocabulary	page 19
W5	Recognition of Text Organization	pages 31, 47, 79
W6	Recognition of a Purpose for Reading	page 47
A1	Questioning, Clarifying, Predicting	page 47
A2	Prediction of Tentative Meaning	page 47
A3	Forming of Opinions	page 63
A4	Making Judgments, Drawing Conclusions	page 63
A5	Literary Elements and Textual Conventions	page 79

*The standards presented in this book were created by the New Jersey State Department of Education. Source: New Jersey Assessment of Skills and Knowledge, 2009 *Score Interpretation Manual*, Grades 3-8: October 2009: Copyright © New Jersey Department of Education. For more information, visit the department's website at *www.state.nj.us/education/aps/cccs/math/*.

Chapter 1

Main Idea and Supporting Details

Clusters

W1   Recognition of a Central Idea or Theme   A central idea or theme is a statement broad enough to cover the entire scope of the reading passage. The central idea or theme may be stated or implied, but clues to it are found in the ideas that tend to recur in the text. Examples of a central idea or theme statement:

Imagination helps us to solve problems.

Ordinary objects can be used to create unusual art.

W2   Recognition of Supporting Details   These questions focus on meaningful details that contribute to the development of a character or the plot or that develop ideas and information that are essential to the central idea of a text.

Main Idea

In this chapter, you'll learn how to find the main idea of a story or article and how to find supporting details. The **main idea** is what a story or article is *mostly* about. Read this paragraph:

1   **Have you ever climbed a tree?**   2   **Have you ever planted a tree?**
3   **Trees are important to the earth.**   4   **Trees look pretty.**   5   **They help keep the air clean.**   6   **They are home to many birds and animals.**
7   **Trees also give people and animals shade.**

1

What is this paragraph mostly about? Did you say trees? Yes! The paragraph is about trees. But let's find a sentence in the paragraph that gives more information about the main idea of the passage. Sentence 1 doesn't tell what the paragraph is mostly about. Neither does sentence 2. Sentence 3 does, however, because all of the sentences after this give details about how trees are important to the earth. See how it works?

Supporting Details

You just learned that details back up the main idea. These details are called **supporting details**. They support, or give more information about, the main idea. Using a web like the one shown below can help you find supporting details. Notice that the main idea of the paragraph about trees is in the center circle. One supporting detail has been included in a circle to help you get started. Fill in the rest of the circles with supporting details from the paragraph about trees.

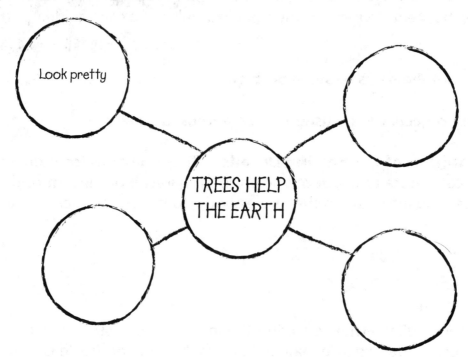

Theme

Fiction, or made-up stories, usually has a theme. The theme is a lot like the main idea. The **theme** is the message or lesson in the story. You usually can't put your finger on a sentence stating the theme. You have to look at the supporting details to figure out the theme. (This is sometimes also true with the main idea. Sometimes you can't put your finger on a sentence stating the main idea. Sometimes you have to figure it out yourself.) Read this story about a boy named Tommy.

Practice Passage: "One Happy Kid"

One Happy Kid

Tommy's room was something to see. He never made his bed. In fact, he sometimes used his bed for other things. He kept some books under his covers. He kept some socks under there, too. And he liked to throw his clothes on top of his bed. Tommy liked to do this a lot. Lots of clothes were on his bed. And Tommy usually just slept on top of them.

But the floor of Tommy's room was even worse than his bed. Many papers were on the floor. So many papers were on the floor that you couldn't really see the carpet. Tommy liked to eat in his room, too. So there were dishes on the floor. And cups. And even a banana peel. Lots of broken toys were on the floor, too. Tommy said that some of them still worked. But no one knew for sure.

Tommy looked a mess, too. He rarely combed his hair. And he refused to get a haircut. He usually had some kind of food on his face. And he never tied his shoes. In fact, sometimes his shoes didn't match. And when Tommy wore socks, they didn't match, either. "Tommy, really now, what am I going to do with you?" his mother often asked. But Tommy would just grin from ear to ear. He was one happy kid.

Now answer this question:

What is a theme of "One Happy Kid"?

    Ⓐ Some kids are very happy.

    Ⓑ Some kids are very messy.

    Ⓒ Tommy looks a mess.

    Ⓓ Tommy has food on his face.

There are many supporting details in this story. You need to choose the answer choice that *most* of these details support. Remember that the theme, like the main idea, should be about the whole story. Most of the details in the story support the idea that Tommy is messy. He is happy, but this is not the theme of the story, so answer choice A is not correct. Answer choice B seems like a good answer. Just about all of the details support the idea that some kids can be very messy. Do you know a kid like Tommy? You probably do. Answer choice B is a very good answer. Answer choice C is not correct, because many of the details are about Tommy's room, and not just Tommy. The same is true of answer choice D. This is a supporting detail and not the theme. Answer choice B is the best answer.

Now write five supporting details—details about how Tommy is messy—on the lines below.

· Tommy has food on is face.
· Tommy has papers on the floor.
· Tommy has clothes on his bed.
· Tommy dosen't tie his shoes.
· Tommy has shoes that dosen't match.

Passage 1

Read the poem below. Then answer the questions about the poem. Use the hints underneath each question to help you choose the right answer.

Little Kittens

Anonymous (circa 1880)

Two little kittens, one stormy night,
Began to quarrel, and then to fight;
One had a mouse, the other had none,
And that's the way the quarrel begun.

"I'll have that mouse," said the biggest cat;
"You'll have that mouse? We'll see about that!"
"I will have that mouse," said the eldest son;
"You shan't have the mouse," said the little one.

I told you before 'twas a stormy night
When these two little kittens began to fight;
The old woman seized her sweeping broom,
And swept the two kittens right out of the room.

The ground was covered with frost and snow,
And the two little kittens had nowhere to go;
So they laid them down on the mat at the door,
While the old woman finished sweeping the floor.

Then they crept in, as quiet as mice,
All wet with the snow, and cold as ice,
For they found it was better, that stormy night,
To lie down and sleep than to quarrel and fight.

 **Questions**

1. **What were the two kittens fighting about?**

   Ⓐ the snow

   Ⓑ a broom

   Ⓒ a mouse

   Ⓓ the frost

   💡 HINT

   This question asks about a supporting detail. If you're not sure of the answer, reread the poem.

2. What did the old woman do to the kittens?

Ⓐ told them to be quiet

Ⓑ made them go to sleep

Ⓒ swept them outside

Ⓓ told them not to fight

 HINT

This question also asks about a supporting detail. If you're not sure of the answer, reread the poem. How did the kittens get outside?

3. What is a theme of "Little Kittens"?

Ⓐ Listen to your mother.

Ⓑ It is good to get along.

Ⓒ It is cold outside at night.

Ⓓ Friends should help each other.

 HINT

This question asks about the theme. What lesson did the kittens learn? How did they act when they came back inside?

Passage 2

Read the passage below. Then answer the questions. Use the hints underneath each question to help you choose the right answer.

The Man with a Bright Idea: Thomas Edison

The only time most of us think about lightbulbs is when it's time to get a new one. Lightbulbs are inside many different things. There are bulbs in lamps, stoplights, and even cars. What would life be like without the lightbulb? Of course, people didn't always have lightbulbs. Instead, they used candles and gas lamps to see during the night. That all changed when a man named Thomas Edison made the first useful lightbulb.

Thomas was the youngest of seven children. As a child, Thomas had a sickness that caused him to lose all of his hearing in one ear. This illness caused Thomas to start school late. Thomas did not like going to school very much. He was often thinking about other things while he should have been listening to his teacher. After three months, Thomas's mom decided to teach him at home. She showed him how to read and write. Thomas learned to love reading. He read almost any book. Soon Thomas became interested in learning how things worked. When his parents couldn't explain how something worked, Thomas tried to find out on his own.

Soon Thomas started to invent things. This means that he made new things or made other things better. By the age of 12, Thomas had also started his own business. Thomas sold a newspaper to people riding on the train. As he grew up, Thomas had many jobs near the train station. Sometimes he sold candy and snacks to hungry passengers. One day, Thomas saw a little boy on the train tracks. Thomas pulled him to safety. The boy's father thanked Thomas for saving his son.

The man offered Thomas another job. For this job, Thomas learned how to use a telegraph. Before there were telephones, telegraphs were used to send messages from one place to another. The messages were sent using a number of taps. Each tap was used to replace a letter in the alphabet. The person on the other end would listen to the taps and turn them into the right words. Thomas needed to listen very carefully to all of the taps. If he didn't, he might not get the message right. The fact that Thomas could only hear out of one ear helped him with his job. Because Thomas could only hear out of one ear, he couldn't hear the other things going on around him. This made it easier for him to get the message correct.

Thomas became very good at his job. What Thomas really wanted to do was invent things. Working all day did not give him the time that he needed to make his ideas come to life. Thomas later fixed broken machines for a large business in New York. Soon Thomas made enough money to leave his job and spend all of his time inventing.

He moved his family to New Jersey. There he spent much of his time coming up with new ideas. His first big invention was a phonograph. A phonograph was the first machine that recorded sound and played it back. The phonograph was sort of like the first CD player. Back then, the phonograph seemed like magic to most people.

Though this was an important invention, it is not what Thomas would become famous for. Thomas worked hard to figure out how to make an electric lightbulb. He spent a lot of time and money on this project. Finally, he got it right. Though many other people were trying to make lightbulbs, Thomas's idea ended up being the best. This was because his lightbulbs lasted longer. Thomas also wanted to make lightbulbs that were not too expensive. Thomas became known across the country and around the world.

Questions

1. **What is this passage mostly about?**

   Ⓐ Thomas Edison's life

   Ⓑ the first lightbulb

   Ⓒ the things Thomas made

   Ⓓ Thomas Edison's jobs

   HINT

   This question asks you to find what the whole passage is about. Choose the answer choice that tells what the entire passage is about.

2. **What did Thomas do when he was 12 years old?**

   Ⓐ learn to read

   Ⓑ learn to use a telegraph

   Ⓒ start his own business

   Ⓓ sell candy and snacks

   HINT

   The answer to this question is right in the passage. Look for the paragraph that tells what Thomas did when he was 12 years old.

3. **The second paragraph of this passage is mostly about**

   Ⓐ Thomas's life as a boy.

   Ⓑ how Thomas got sick.

   Ⓒ how Thomas learned to read.

   Ⓓ Thomas's school.

HINT

Reread the second paragraph. Think about what most of the sentences are about.

4. **What was Thomas's first big invention?**

   Ⓐ the lightbulb

   Ⓑ the telegraph

   Ⓒ the telephone

   Ⓓ the phonograph

HINT

This question is about a supporting detail. Reread the passage if you're not sure of the correct answer.

Passage 3

Read the story below. Then answer the questions about the story. Use the hints underneath each question to help you choose the right answer.

The Lion and the Mouse

adapted from Aesop's Fables

Once upon a time, Lion, the King of Beasts, was sound asleep in a field. A little mouse scampered across the field. Without even realizing it, Mouse ran back and forth across Lion's back. Mouse's little claws were very sharp, and they dug into the skin beneath Lion's fur.

Suddenly, Lion's eyes opened wide, and he placed one of his large paws on top of Mouse. Mouse was trapped. Then Lion grabbed Mouse by the tail and held him up in the air.

"What is the meaning of this?" Lion asked angrily. "Why did you wake me?"

The little mouse trembled with fear. "I . . . I . . . I am so very sorry. I did not mean to wake you," the mouse said.

Lion raised his eyebrows. "I don't believe you," he said. Then he opened his powerful jaws and moved Mouse closer to his mouth.

"Please don't eat me!" Mouse begged. "If you let me go, I will never forget your kindness. I may even be able to help *you* someday."

When the lion heard this, he threw back his big head and laughed loudly. "What could *you*, a little mouse, possibly do for *me*, the King of Beasts?"

Mouse did not know what to say. "Friends help each other," he said. "A little friend is a good thing to have."

Lion kept on laughing. "I'll tell you what," he said. "You made me laugh. You are a funny little mouse. I'm not going to eat you. I will set you free."

Lion gently set Mouse on the ground. He watched as the little mouse quickly scampered away into the tall grass.

Then one day hunters came into the forest. "Hunters!" Crow shouted. "We are in great danger! Run away quickly and hide!" Most of the animals heard Crow and did what he said. But not Lion. He thought he was too tough for the hunters. *They can't hurt* me, *the King of Beasts*, he thought.

The hunters set traps made of netting on the ground under trees. When an animal stepped on the ground below the trees, the trap would fall on top of it and quickly pull the trapped animal up high in the air.

Lion roared loudly. He thought that the hunters would run if they heard his powerful roar. But then Lion stepped into one of the hunters' traps. He yelled loudly as he became trapped in the net and pulled up high off the ground. "I am trapped!" he yelled. "Someone help me now!"

But none of the animals were around except for Mouse. "I'll help you," Mouse said. "Hang on, my friend." Mouse scampered up the tree and jumped onto the net. Using his very sharp little teeth, he chewed hard.

"Hurry!" Lion said. "I think I hear the hunters." Mouse chewed and chewed until he had made a hole in the net large enough for Lion to fit through. "Run!" Mouse shouted. Lion jumped out of the net and ran deep into the forest. When he was safe in his den, he thought about what Mouse had done for him. "Friends help each other," he said, "and a little friend is a good thing to have."

 Questions

1. **How does Mouse help Lion?**

   Ⓐ Mouse makes Lion laugh.

   Ⓑ Mouse tells Lion about danger.

   Ⓒ Mouse looks for Lion in the forest.

   Ⓓ Mouse sets Lion free from a trap.

HINT

This question asks about a supporting detail. Reread the end of the story. How does Mouse help Lion? Remember that Lion is surprised that an animal so small could help him.

2. **Who warns the animals in the forest about the hunters?**

   Ⓐ Rabbit

   Ⓑ Mouse

   Ⓒ Lion

   Ⓓ Crow

HINT

This question also asks about a supporting detail. If you don't know the answer to this question, reread the story.

3. **What is a theme of "The Lion and the Mouse"?**

   Use information from the story to support your response. Write your answer on the lines below.

The theme "The Lion and the Mouse."
This is a story about a lion and a mouse who
lived in the forest. One day, the mouse climbed
over a sleeping lion. The lion hold the mouse
in his paw want to eat it. The mouse begged for
mercury and said "Please let me go I will help
you in the furture when you need help. The
lion thought and the mouse go free. Another
day, the lion was trapped in a hunter's net.
The lion roared and cried for help. The mouse
came to It's rescue. He nibbled the net and
set the lion free. The lion quickly jumped out
of the net and went into it's cave. The lion
learned a lesson. He learned that friend's
help each other no matter how big or
small the are.

HINT

Think about the lesson Lion learns from Mouse.
Reread the end of the story for a clue.

Chapter 2

Understanding New Words

Clusters

W4 Paraphrasing/Vocabulary   These questions on the NJ ASK focus on the meaning of words used in the text and elicit students' use of effective reading strategies to determine the meaning. Targeted vocabulary always occurs within a semantic and syntactic context that students should draw on to respond to the question.

New Words

What do you do when you are reading and come across a new word? Do you look up the word in a dictionary? Do you skip over the new word and keep on reading? If you're like most people, you probably try to figure out the meaning of the new word by looking at the words around it. This is called looking for **context clues**. On the NJ ASK, you may be asked to choose the meaning of some words that are new to you. You can usually figure out the meaning of these words by looking at the context clues.

Read this sentence:

Put the <u>skilly-wag</u> in the lock and then open the door.

What's a skilly-wag? A skilly-wag is a just a made-up word. But you can tell from the words "lock" and "door" that it is some kind of key.

Let's try another one:

"That ice cream is starting to melt!" Mom yelled. "Hurry up and put it in the <u>diddly-do</u>."

What do you think a diddly-do is? The words "ice cream" and "melt" are clues that it is a kind of freezer.

Now you try it:

> **"Kathy," Ms. Diaz said, "please raise your <u>pasecki</u> before asking a question. It is rude to call out."**

What's a pasecki?

A pasecki is ones hand.

What words in the sentence offered clues?

The words "raise" and "rude" offered clues.

Words with More Than One Meaning

Some words have more than one meaning. This can make it even harder to figure out their meaning. Always look at the context—that is, the words and sentences around the word—before choosing an answer choice. The following sentences contain words with more than one meaning:

> **The <u>wind</u> is blowing outside.**

> **<u>Wind</u> your alarm clock before you go to bed.**

> **Put the chickens in their <u>pen</u>.**

> **Use this <u>pen</u> to write your essay.**

Practice Poem

Now read this poem and answer the question.

At the Seaside

by Robert Louis Stevenson

When I was down beside the sea

A wooden spade they gave to me

To dig the sandy shore.

My holes were empty like a cup,

In every hole the sea came up,

Till it could come no more.

What does the word "spade" mean in this poem?

Ⓐ stick

Ⓑ rock

Ⓒ bucket

Ⓓ shovel

The words "wooden" and "dig" in the poem offer clues. While you could dig with a stick, this is probably not the best answer choice. You could probably also dig with a rock, but not very well. You can't dig so well with a bucket, either—but you can dig well with a shovel, as it's made to help you do just that! Answer choice D is the best answer.

Passage 1

Read the poem below. Then answer the questions about the poem. Use the hints underneath each question to help you choose the right answer.

My Shadow

by Robert Louis Stevenson

I have a little shadow that goes in and out with me,
And what can be the use of him is more than I can see.
He is very, very like me from the heels up to the head;
And I see him jump before me, when I jump into my bed.

The funniest thing about him is the way he likes to grow—
Not at all like proper children, which is always very slow;
For he sometimes shoots up taller like an India-rubber ball,
And he sometimes goes so little that there's none of him at all.

He hasn't got a notion of how children ought to play,
And can only make a fool of me in every sort of way.
He stays so close behind me, he's a coward you can see;
I'd think shame to stick to nursie as that shadow sticks to me!

One morning, very early, before the sun was up,
I rose and found the shining dew on every buttercup;
But my lazy little shadow, like an arrant sleepy-head,
Had stayed at home behind me and was fast asleep in bed.

 **Questions**

1. What does the word "proper" mean in these lines from the poem: "The funniest thing about him is the way he likes to grow— / Not at all like proper children, which is always very slow"?

   Ⓐ most

   Ⓑ big

   Ⓒ loud

   Ⓓ funny

   HINT

   Try taking out the word "proper." Then put each answer choice in place of the word. Choose the one that makes the most sense.

2. What does the word "notion" mean in the third stanza of the poem?

   Ⓐ a thought

   Ⓑ a sight

   Ⓒ a clue

   Ⓓ a friend

   HINT

   It always helps to cross off answer choices that you know are not right. Then choose the one that is the best answer.

3. What does the word "sort" mean in this line from the poem: "And can only make a fool of me in every sort of way"?

   Ⓐ mean

   Ⓑ large

   Ⓒ kind

   Ⓓ place

   HINT

   Take the word out of the sentence. Then put each answer choice in place of the word. This will help you find the best answer.

Passage 2

Read the story below. Then answer the questions about the story. Use the hints underneath each question to help you choose the right answer.

Excerpt from *Black Beauty*

by Anna Sewell

The first place that I can well remember was a pleasant meadow with a pond of clear water in it. Over the hedge on one side we looked into a plowed field, and on the other we looked over a gate at our master's house, which stood by the roadside. While I was young I lived upon my mother's milk, as I could not eat grass. In the daytime I ran by her side, and at night I lay down close by her. When it was hot we used to stand by the pond in the shade of the trees, and when it was cold we had a warm shed near the grove.

There were six young colts in the meadow beside me; they were older than I was. I used to run with them, and had great fun; we used to gallop all together round the field, as hard as we could go. Sometimes we had rather rough play, for they would bite and kick, as well as gallop.

One day, when there was a good deal of kicking, my mother whinnied to me to come to her, and then she said: "I wish you to pay attention to what I am going to say. The colts who live here are very good colts, but they are cart-horse colts, and they have not learned manners. You have been well-bred and well-born; your father has a great name in these parts, and your grandfather won the cup at the races; your grandmother had the sweetest temper of any horse I ever knew, and I think you have never seen me kick or bite. I hope you will grow up gentle and good, and never learn bad ways; do your work with a good will, lift your feet up well when you trot, and never bite or kick even in play."

I have never forgotten my mother's advice. I knew she was a wise old horse, and our master thought a great deal of her. Her name was Duchess, but he called her Pet.

Our master was a good, kind man. He gave us good food, good lodging and kind words; he spoke as kindly to us as he did to his little children. We were all fond of him, and my mother loved him very much. When she saw him at the gate she would neigh with joy, and trot up to him. He would pat and stroke her and say, "Well, old Pet, and how is your little Darkie?" I was a dull black, so he called me Darkie; then he would give me a piece of bread, which was very good, and sometimes he brought a carrot for my mother. All the horses would come to him, but I think we were his favorites. My mother always took him to town on a market-day in a light gig.

We had a ploughboy, Dick, who sometimes came into our field to pluck blackberries from the hedge. When he had eaten all he wanted he would have what he called fun with the colts, throwing stones and sticks at them to make them gallop. We did not much mind him, for we could gallop off; but sometimes a stone would hit and hurt us.

One day he was at this game, and did not know that the master was in the next field, watching what was going on; over the hedge he jumped in a snap, and catching Dick by the arm, he gave him such a box on the ear as made him roar with the pain and surprise. As soon as we saw the master we trotted up nearer to see what went on.

"Bad boy!" he said, "bad boy! to chase the colts. This is not the first time, nor the second, but it shall be the last. There—take your money and go home; I shall not want you on my farm again." So we never saw Dick any more. Old Daniel, the man who looked after the horses, was just as gentle as our master; so we were well off.

Questions

1. **What does the word "whinnied" mean in the following sentence: "One day, when there was a good deal of kicking, my mother whinnied to me to come to her"?**

    Ⓐ told

    Ⓑ cried

    Ⓒ looked

    Ⓓ knew

    HINT

    Read the sentences around the sentence with the word. Is the mother upset when she says this? Also, try substituting the answer choices in place of the word "whinnied" in the sentence.

2. **In the fifth paragraph, the word "fond" means**

    Ⓐ enjoyed.

    Ⓑ listened.

    Ⓒ liked.

    Ⓓ saw.

    HINT

    Pay close attention to the context clues in this sentence.

3. **What does the word "pluck" mean in the following sentence: "We had a ploughboy, Dick, who sometimes came into our field to pluck blackberries from the hedge"?**

    Ⓐ eat

    Ⓑ pat

    Ⓒ pick

    Ⓓ cook

    HINT

    Try substituting each answer choice in the sentence.

Passage 3

Nature Newsletter

Volume 1, Issue 1

"Clean Up New Jersey" Contest!

By Joe Young

Calling all kids! New Jersey is holding a contest for kids in grades 3 through 6. Kids in schools across the state are asked to sign up for the state cleanup contest. Each school will pick up garbage from the sidewalks and roads in their towns. The school that picks up the most garbage will win a special award for their school! Students should ask their teachers to sign up their schools for the contest. All classes must have two teachers with them when collecting garbage. The teachers will count the number of bags that students gather. Remember that all students should use gloves. Please take the bags to the recycling center. To enter, send a letter to this address:

Mrs. Lynn Gary

1233 School Road
Trenton, NJ 08601

Good luck to all of you!

Can Squirrels Really Fly?

By Sammy Ross

You have probably seen many squirrels outside your house. But did you know that some squirrels can fly? When you think about animals that can fly, you might think of feathers and wings. Flying squirrels don't have any of these things. So, just how do they fly? Well, flying squirrels don't really fly the way that birds do. They glide through the air. This means that the squirrel cannot stay in the air for very long. This is because they do not have wings to flap. Flying squirrels have folds of skin that go from their tiny hands to their back legs. These folds allow the squirrels to jump very far. This helps keep them safe from other animals. Many flying squirrels live in New Jersey. However, you may have never seen one. This is because flying squirrels only come out at night. This is the best time for them to find food. It also makes it easier for them to stay away from other animals that might hurt them. So, next time you see a squirrel, remember that there are some squirrels that can soar!

INSIDE THIS ISSUE

Recycling Questions

Q: What is recycling?

A: Think about the things that we throw away every day. What happens to them? Most of our garbage sits in piles for years. This is not good for our earth! The good news is that many of the things we throw away can be reused. Bottles, cans, and paper can be recycled. This means that all of these things can be used to make new stuff.

Q: How do I recycle?

A: Here's what to do. Get a grown-up to help you. Have three bins at your house. Make one bin for paper. Make another for bottles. Use the third bin for cans. Every time you are finished using one of these things, put it in the bin where it belongs, instead of throwing it away. Ask the grown-up to find out when your town picks up these things.

Q: How does recycling help?

A: Recycling helps in many ways. We make less garbage when we recycle. This helps keep the earth clean and keeps all of us healthy. It can also help save trees from being cut down. The more paper we reuse, the more trees we can save.

Q: Can we recycle at school?

A: Of course! Ask your teacher for help. He or she might think that putting bins in the lunchroom would be helpful. After this is done, you can help show other kids in your class what things go in each bin.

Q: Where can I learn more?

A: There are lots of great books and websites that can give you more information! Check out your school's library. Ask a grown-up to go online with you to find out more about recycling in your town or city.

Questions

1. **What does the word "award" mean in the following sentence: "The school that picks up the most garbage will win a special award for their school"?**

   Ⓐ sign

   Ⓑ prize

   Ⓒ thing

   Ⓓ day

 HINT

Think about what a school that collects the most of something would win.

2. In "Can Squirrels Really Fly?" the word "glide" means

Ⓐ flap.

Ⓑ move.

Ⓒ sail.

Ⓓ bounce.

HINT

An airplane can glide. When it's gliding in the air, what does it do? Look for the best answer choice.

3. What does the word "reused" mean in the following sentence: "The good news is that many of the things we throw away can be reused"?

Ⓐ will use

Ⓑ have used

Ⓒ use first

Ⓓ use again

HINT

The prefix "re-" means "to do the action again."

Chapter 3

Following Directions

Clusters

W5 Recognition of Text Organization   Text organization encompasses the patterns or organization that characterize the respective genres. For everyday texts, questions address structural features such as section topics, charts, and illustrations, in addition to patterns of organization within the text (such as sequence, comparison-contrast, or cause-effect).

W3 Extrapolation of Information   These questions focus on ideas and information that are implied by, but not explicit in, the text.

Introduction

The everyday texts on the NJ ASK are often passages with steps or directions. You need to be able to follow these directions to answer the questions that follow them. You will also have to pay close attention to the way the passage is organized. For example, passages may have steps in them. These passages might have headings such as "Step 1" and "Step 2." These passages might also have pictures. These pictures show you how to do something.

Suppose you want to make a banana milk shake. What kind of book would you look in to learn how to do this? A cookbook? A cookbook is a good choice. A cookbook has many recipes. These recipes tell you how to make food step by step.

Practice Passage

Read this recipe for a banana milk shake and answer the questions that follow.

The World's Best Banana Milk Shake

What you need:

1 frozen banana, peeled

1 cup milk

Blender

Step 1: Peel a fresh banana, and then put it in the freezer. Doing this will keep it fresh. A frozen banana will also make your milk shake colder.

Step 2: Slice the frozen banana into small pieces. Put the pieces in the blender. Add one cup of milk.

Step 3 Mix on medium. If mixture is too thick, add more milk. If it is too thin, add another banana.

Step 4: Enjoy!

⁇ Questions ⁇

1. **The purpose of the first step is to**

   Ⓐ teach you how to keep a banana fresh.

   Ⓑ tell you how to make your milk shake cold.

   Ⓒ give a summary of how to make a milk shake.

   Ⓓ tell you to peel and freeze the banana.

Read each of these answer choices carefully. The purpose of Step 1 is not to keep a banana fresh. It also isn't to tell you how to make the milk shake cold. It isn't a summary, either. Answer choice D is the best. Step 1 tells you to peel and freeze the banana.

3.5
/4

2.   What is the purpose of the blender? Write your answer on the lines below.

The purpose of the blender is making shakes of a fruit crushed and really yummy and it really makes it refreshing. In the story the author states " Peel a fresh banana and then put it, In the freezer. Doing this will keep it fresh. A frozen banana will also make your milk shake colder. Enjoy." This shows what the purpose of the blender is about. This small recipe about the best banana shake to a story called "How To Make The World's Best Apple Shake Ever Tasted" because it talks about the recipe. It talks about how to make an apple shake and it's steps to make an apple shake. That's how that story I read is similiar to this recipe. That's also I how compared these stories.

Passage 1

Read the passage below. Then answer the questions about the passage. Use the hints underneath each question to help you choose the right answer.

How to Fly a Kite

Have you ever flown a kite? Flying a kite is a lot of fun, but it's not as easy as you may think.

You need to wait for a good day to fly a kite. There has to be some wind, since wind is what makes a kite fly. It can't be too windy, however. If it is too windy, the string on your kite will snap. You'll lose your kite if this happens. A medium wind is best. Make sure that it is bright and sunny outside. Never fly a kite in bad weather.

You need to go to an open area to fly a kite. You need lots of flying space to fly a kite. Stay away from trees and power lines. Your kite might be tangled in these. Also stay away from roads. You need to stay safe when flying your kite. Always take a grown-up with you in case you need help.

When you're just learning to a fly a kite, you should start with a very basic kite. This type of kite looks like a triangle with a tail. Fancy kites are harder to fly. Make sure your kite string is wrapped around a spool.

To fly your kite, stand with your back to the wind. Hold your kite up straight and let the line out. If the wind is good, your kite will lift right up into the air. If not, you might have to run a little while holding the string. Drag the kite behind you. Or you can have a grown-up hold the kite while you run. This is usually enough to get the kite off the ground.

Figure 1

You will have to let out the string as your kite sails in the air. The more string you let out, the higher your kite will fly. Be careful not to let out too much string! If you do, your kite might crash to the ground. If your kite begins to drop, stop letting out string.

If you move while holding the string, you kite will move, too. This is the fun part. If you move the string up and down, you can make your kite dance!

To land your kite, you simply wind up the string and bring the kite in toward you. When the kite is close enough so that you can reach it, pull it down.

After you have flown your kite a few times, you can make some changes. If your kite flies too slowly, you can shorten its tail. And if it flies too fast, add a longer tail.

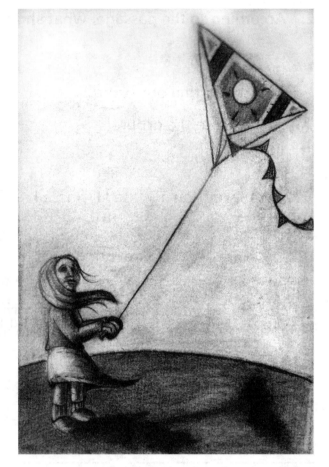

Figure 2

 Questions

1. **The purpose of Figure 1 in this passage is to show you**

   Ⓐ how to run with a kite.

   Ⓑ how to land a kite.

   Ⓒ how to hold a kite.

   Ⓓ what a kite looks like.

 HINT

Look carefully at Figure 1. What is the person doing?

2. **According to the passage, what should you do if your kite starts to go down?**

   Ⓐ Run with it.

   Ⓑ Stop letting out string.

   Ⓒ Pull it to the ground.

   Ⓓ Turn around.

HINT

Find this part of the passage and reread it.

3. **Explain how to land a kite. Use information from the article to support your response. Write your answer on the lines below.**

To land a kite, pull the string towards you. When it comes close to you can also catch it.

Passage 2

Read the passage below. Then answer the questions about the passage. Use the hints underneath each question to help you choose the right answer.

How to Make a Sock Puppet

Do you or your parents have a lot of old socks in a drawer? Have those socks lost their mates long ago? Don't throw them away. Save them for a rainy day—and make sock puppets!

What you'll need:

An old, clean sock

Glue

Scissors

Cloth scraps or felt

Cardboard or poster board

Construction paper

An adult to help you cut

Step 1: Put the sock on your hand and bend your wrist. Your fingers should be in the toe of the sock, and the back of your wrist should be in the heel of the sock. See how your hand forms the head of your puppet. Think about what kind of animal you will make out of your sock.

Step 2: Press your fingers and thumb together, and then separate them. Have an adult use scissors to cut a slit in the sock between your fingers and your thumb to begin making the puppet's mouth.

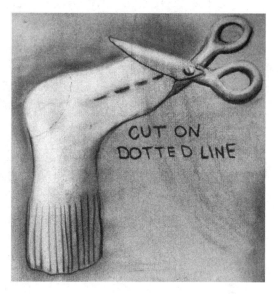

Step 3: Cut an oval out of cardboard, poster board, or other stiff paper. Make your oval about five inches long and about three inches wide.

Step 4: Choose a piece of cloth to be the inside of your puppet's mouth. Lay the cardboard oval on the fabric and trace it with a marker. Then cut out the oval from the cloth.

Step 5: Glue the cloth oval to the cardboard oval. Let the glue dry before you fold the oval in half.

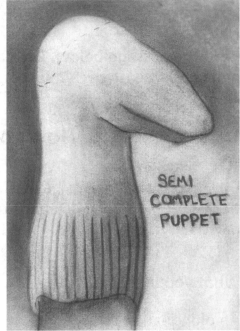

SEMI COMPLETE PUPPET

Step 6: Lay your sock flat so that the slit you cut is facing upward. Place the oval inside the slit so that the colorful side of the oval is showing. Now glue the edges of the sock to the edges of the oval.

Step 7: When the glue is dry, slide your hand into the sock puppet. Put your fingers in the top part of the mouth and your thumb should be in the bottom part. Open and close your puppet's mouth to make it talk.

Step 8: Cut out two one-inch circles of a light-colored cloth, and then cut two tiny circles from a dark-colored cloth. Glue a dark circle in the center of each light circle. These will be your puppet's eyes. Place the eyes on the puppet and glue them in place.

Step 9: Think about what kind of animal your sock puppet will be. This may depend on what you have to work with. Here are some things to think about:

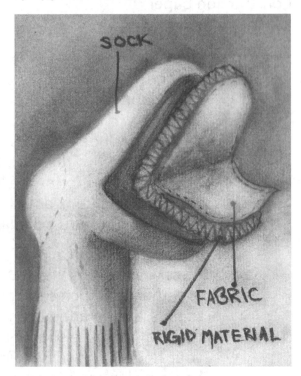

SOCK

FABRIC

RIGID MATERIAL

- You can stuff fabric with cotton balls to make arms, and have an adult sew the arms onto your puppet for you.

- You can make big, floppy dog ears or small, pointy pig ears.

- You can give your puppet a silly, hanging tongue or a mouth full of teeth.

- You can glue small triangles along the head and neck of your puppet to make a dragon.

- You can cut out cloth wings and have an adult sew them on for you to make a bird puppet.

- You can make long cardboard rabbit ears and use pipe cleaners for whiskers.

You can make just about any kind of puppet you can imagine—or you can make one of each! If your friends make puppets, too, you can all put on a puppet show. Sock puppets can be lots of fun!

Questions

1. **What material is used to make the puppet's mouth?**

   Ⓐ cloth

   Ⓑ paper

   Ⓒ glue

   Ⓓ cardboard

 HINT

Reread Step 4.

2. **The purpose of Step 8 is to tell you**

    Ⓐ how to make the eyes.

    Ⓑ how to make the mouth.

    Ⓒ where to put the glue.

    Ⓓ what kind of felt to use.

HINT

Reread Step 8. Choose the answer choice that tells what the entire step is about.

3. **What should you add to your sock puppet to make it look like a dragon?**

    Ⓐ cotton balls

    Ⓑ cloth wings

    Ⓒ hanging tongue

    Ⓓ small triangles

HINT

Reread Step 9.

Passage 3

Read the passage below. Then answer the questions about the passage. Use the hints underneath each question to help you choose the right answer.

How to Have Your Own Treasure Hunt

Maybe you've heard stories about grown-ups who follow puzzling maps to find strange fortunes. Perhaps you've seen a movie where a brave person goes away on a wild adventure. Have you ever wished that you and your friends could have such a journey?

To have your own treasure hunt, all you need are a friend or two, some paper, and something that your friend treasures!

Step 1: Invite a friend over.

The great thing about a Treasure Hunt is that you don't have to go outside to do it, so it's a wonderful project for a rainy or snowy day. But it makes a good outside game too! Call a friend or two and let them know you're planning a Treasure Hunt just for them. Tell them when they should come over. You'll probably need about an hour to put everything in place.

Step 2: Gather your supplies.

First of all, you'll need a treasure. Many treasure stories have a chest of gold at the end of the trail, but your treasure doesn't have to be so over-the-top. Anything is a treasure if someone works for it. Use your imagination. Your treasure could be a free pass to go first the next time you play a game together. Your treasure could be a book that you're done reading but your friends have been eager to get their hands on. What would bring a smile to your friends' faces? Let that be your treasure.

You'll need a few sheets of paper and something to write with. Don't forget the most important part—you must have a good imagination.

> ## What You'll Need
>
> a treasure
> some paper and pens
> imagination

Step 3: Pick your starting point.

Everything has to start somewhere, even a treasure hunt. Pick a good hiding place for your starting point. Don't pick a place that your friends will never be able to find, but you don't want your starting point out in the open either.

Step 4: Write your opening clue.

A clue is a just a couple of sentences that will help your friends find their treasure. Your opening clue should let the reader know that a treasure hunt is beginning. You might try something like the note shown here:

Later, after you welcome the treasure hunters to the game, you will continue by telling them where to look first. Here is an example of what you might write:

Clouds are white.
The sky is blue.
This treasure hunt
was made for you.

This hunt starts
where you like to sit.
Look for a place
your hand might fit.

Does that sound puzzling? You'll find out what it means soon. For now, put your opening clue aside and move on.

Step 5: Pick your hiding spots.

Look around and pick a few more hiding spots. They don't have to be close together, but you should stay in a small area so that your friends will have only a certain space to search, or else this hunt will take all day!

Step 6: Write your clues.

Next, write another clue. Remember that each clue should lead the hunters to the next clue. Say you want to hide a clue in a plant. How would you describe the plant without giving the hiding spot away too easily? How about the note shown here:

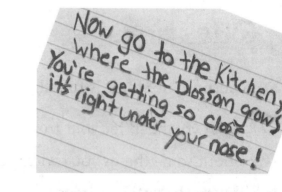

Now go to the Kitchen, where the blossom grows. You're getting so close its right under your nose!

Clues don't have to rhyme, but they can. They don't even have to be words. You could draw pictures that lead your friends to the next clue. Use your imagination and have fun!

Step 7: Set it all up.

Once you've picked your hiding spots and written your clues, hide all of your clues. Remember that you will be giving your friends the opening clue, so keep that handy. Our opening clue looked like the top of the note shown here:

Clouds are white. The sky is blue. This treasure hunt was made for you.

This hunt starts where you like to sit. Look for a place your hand might fit.

Hide your next clue wherever the opening clue leads. In this example, it would be hidden under the seat of a friend's favorite chair.

Keep hiding all of the clues. Each clue should lead to the next hiding spot. You can have as many clues as you like, but the final clue should lead to the treasure.

Step 8: Hunt!

When your friends arrive, hand one friend the opening clue, stand back, and enjoy!

Your friends will be excited to find the treasure, but most of the fun is in the hunt. You might find when you're done that you want to enjoy the hunt all over again. Just give your friends these directions and some free time. Next, <u>you'll</u> get to have a treasure hunt!

Questions

1. **The purpose of Step 2 is to tell you**

   Ⓐ what you need for your treasure hunt.

   Ⓑ about some things you can use as treasure.

   Ⓒ where to start your treasure hunt.

   Ⓓ what treasure stories use as treasure.

HINT

Reread Step 2. Choose the answer choice that tells what it is mostly about. This is the reason the author included it.

2. **The purpose of the picture with Step 1 is to**

   Ⓐ show that a phone can be treasure.

   Ⓑ show you how to get started.

   Ⓒ teach you how to use the phone.

   Ⓓ tell you to call your friends.

HINT

Reread Step 1 carefully. What is this step mostly about?

3. **Explain how to write your opening clue. Use information from the article to support your answer. Write your answer on the lines below.**

You have an opening clue when you let the reader know the treasure hunt has started. In step 4, It talks about the beginning. This shows how step 4 talks about opening clues.

R
A
C
E

💡 HINT

Reread the part of the passage that tells how to write your opening clue.

4. **Where should you start your treasure hunt? Use information from the article to support your answer. Write your answer on the lines below.**

You should start your hunt by hiding the treasure. In Step 3, It gives you advice about how you should hide it. This proves that I know where to start the hunt after reading this article

HINT

Reread the part of the passage that tells how to start your treasure hunt.

Chapter 4

Author's Purpose and Prediction

Clusters

W6   Recognition of a Purpose for Reading   These questions, which focus on the reader's purpose, address reasons for a particular text. A story, for example, may convey specific information about a species of animal or a culture, although that may not be the primary purpose of the text.

W5   Recognition of Text Organization   Text organization encompasses the patterns of organization that characterize the respective genres. For everyday texts, questions address structural features such as section topics, charts, and illustrations, in addition to patterns of organization within the text (such as sequence, comparison-contrast, or cause-effect).

A1   Questioning, Clarifying, Predicting   These questions draw on students' use of reading strategies to construct meaning. The questions introduce a focus and a context for responding (e.g., asking a question of the author or a character), and ask students to select and analyze ideas and information from the text to develop a response. Given the nature of this task, these questions are almost always open-ended items.

A2   Prediction of Tentative Meaning   These questions focus on statements within the text that introduce some ambiguity: either the ideas are not fully explained or the statement uses language that can be read in two or more ways. For these questions, students use their knowledge of language and of the context within the reading passage to analyze the meaning of a particular statement.

Introduction

Writers write for a reason. Think about the last time you wrote something. Maybe it was a story just for fun. Or maybe you wrote a paragraph for English class. Or maybe you gave a friend directions to your house. Some of the questions on the NJ ASK ask you why an author wrote a passage.

Authors sometimes include charts and maps in their writing. They sometimes also include headings or pictures. All of these things make writing easier to understand. You might be asked why an author included something in a passage on the NJ ASK.

Last, did you ever watch a movie and guess the ending? Sometimes it's helpful to predict what will happen next when you are reading. Some of an author's ideas may not be fully explained. You might be asked to predict an author's meaning.

Author's Purpose

Authors often write for these reasons:

- To make or convince you to do something

- To describe what something is like

- To entertain with a story about characters

- To inform you about something

- To teach you how to do something

Imagine that you wrote your friend a letter trying to get her to try out for the soccer team. The purpose of your letter would be to convince. Now imagine that you wrote your friend a letter to tell what it is like at your grandmother's house. Your purpose then would be to describe. If you wrote a story for fun, your purpose is to entertain. If you write a report about dolphins at the New Jersey State Aquarium, your purpose is to inform. If you write down the steps your friend should take to get from her house to yours, you're teaching your friend how to do something.

Many authors have pictures to go with their writing. Looking at a picture makes something easier to understand. Maps are helpful sometimes, too. Numbers might be easier to understand if a chart is included. You might also be asked on the NJ ASK why an author included something.

Write the purpose for each of the following on the line below it.

1. A letter asking for your money back on something

_____

2. A story about two kids who travel into outer space

_____

3. A paper about the first baseball game, in Hoboken, New Jersey

_____

4. A recipe telling how to make spaghetti sauce

_____

5. A poem telling what it feels like to be outside in the rain

_____

6. A map of your town

_____

Prediction

When you're reading a book, do you like to guess what will happen next? Most people do. When you make a guess, you're making a prediction. On the NJ ASK, you might also be asked to predict in a different way. You might have to predict—or guess—what an author means. For example, imagine an author writes, "Keep the plant in a warm place." How warm is warm? Does the author mean to keep the plant on top of a hot stove? Probably not. The author probably means to keep the plant in a sunny spot in your house that's not cold.

Practice Passage

Read this story and then answer the questions.

The Old House

Abe was playing catch with his younger brothers. They were having a great time. Then Abe threw the ball too far. It landed on the porch of an old house. Abe knew that no one lived in the house anymore. No one had lived in the house in a very long time. The house's windows were broken. And the grass was very high. The house was a mess. But Abe needed the ball back.

Abe opened the old gate to get into the yard. It made a loud creaking sound. Abe took a deep breath. Then he walked up onto the porch and reached for the ball. Just then—

What do you think will happen next? Write your answer on the lines below.

Bats came out flying. He was so shocked by the flapping noise from the bats and he also saw mice running here and there. Abe was so terrified that he ran back to his house. He never thought about going back to that house to fetch his ball.

Passage 1

Read the passage below. Then answer the questions about the passage. Use the hints underneath each question to help you choose the right answer.

Sweet Treat

Have you ever eaten a sweet potato? Sweet potatoes have lots of vitamins and minerals that make you strong and healthy. You can prepare them many ways, and they taste great! Some people boil them, fry them, or bake them. Sometimes sweet potatoes are turned into delicious snacks. You can make sweet potato chips or sweet potato pie. One easy way to cook sweet potatoes is to mash them.

You can buy sweet potatoes at the store or at a farmers' market. Sweet potatoes are red, purple, brown, or white on the outside. Raw, or uncooked, sweet potatoes should be firm, not soft. Also, they shouldn't have any cracks or bruises. If you're not going to cook the potatoes right away, you should store them in a cool, dry place.

To prepare the sweet potatoes, wash them with clean water. Use a potato peeler to remove the skin from the potatoes. The inside of a sweet potato is white, yellow, orange, or purple.

Ask your mother, father, or another adult to help you cut the potatoes into pieces. Your helper should also put them on the stove to boil. The potatoes will be soft when they finish cooking. You should be able to mash them with a fork.

Then it's time to add the finishing touches to make them even more delicious. Drop a little bit of butter into the potatoes. Also add some brown sugar. This will give the potatoes some extra sweetness. The potatoes will still be hot, so the butter and sugar will start to melt. Stir the potatoes to mix in the butter and the sugar. Then serve them to your family or friends!

 Questions

1. **Why did the author write this passage?**

    Ⓐ to inform readers about sweet potatoes

    Ⓑ to convince readers to cook and eat sweet potatoes

    Ⓒ to entertain readers with a story about sweet potatoes

    Ⓓ to describe what a sweet potato looks like

    HINT

    Think about what the entire passage is about. Thinking about this will help you understand why the author wrote it.

2. **With which sentence would the author of this passage most likely agree?**

    Ⓐ Sweet potatoes are good for you.

    Ⓑ Yellow sweet potatoes taste best.

    Ⓒ Sweet potatoes are hard to make.

    Ⓓ Sweet potatoes taste best mashed.

    HINT

    Reread the beginning of the article for a clue.

3. How would a sweet potato taste if you added a lot of brown sugar? Use information from the article to support your answer. Write your answer on the lines below.

_____

_____

_____

_____

_____

_____

_____

_____

_____

_____

_____

_____

_____

 HINT

Reread the end of the passage. How does brown sugar make sweet potatoes taste?

Passage 2

Read the passage below. Then answer the questions about the passage. Use the hints underneath each question to help you choose the right answer.

Excerpt from *The Jungle Book*

by Rudyard Kipling

He was a mongoose, rather like a little cat in his fur and his tail, but quite like a weasel in his head and his habits. His eyes and the end of his restless nose were pink. He could scratch himself anywhere he pleased with any leg, front or back, that he chose to use. He could fluff up his tail till it looked like a bottle brush, and his war cry as he scuttled through the long grass was: "Rikk-tikk-tikki-tikki-tchk!"

One day, a high summer flood washed him out of the burrow where he lived with his father and mother, and carried him, kicking and clucking, down a roadside ditch. He found a little wisp of grass floating there, and clung to it till he lost his senses. When he revived, he was lying in the hot sun on the middle of a garden path, very draggled indeed, and a small boy was saying, "Here's a dead mongoose. Let's have a funeral."

"No," said his mother, "let's take him in and dry him. Perhaps he isn't really dead."

They took him into the house, and a big man picked him up between his finger and thumb and said he was not dead but half choked. So they wrapped him in cotton wool, and warmed him over a little fire, and he opened his eyes and sneezed.

"Now," said the big man (he was an Englishman who had just moved into the bungalow), "don't frighten him, and we'll see what he'll do."

It is the hardest thing in the world to frighten a mongoose, because he is eaten up from nose to tail with curiosity. The motto of all the mongoose family is "Run and find out," and Rikki-tikki was a true mongoose. He looked at the cotton wool, decided that it was not good to eat, ran all round the table, sat up and put his fur in order, scratched himself, and jumped on the small boy's shoulder.

"Don't be frightened, Teddy," said his father. "That's his way of making friends."

"Ouch! He's tickling under my chin," said Teddy.

Rikki-tikki looked down between the boy's collar and neck, snuffed at his ear, and climbed down to the floor, where he sat rubbing his nose.

"Good gracious," said Teddy's mother, "and that's a wild creature! I suppose he's so tame because we've been kind to him."

"All mongooses are like that," said her husband. "If Teddy doesn't pick him up by the tail, or try to put him in a cage, he'll run in and out of the house all day long. Let's give him something to eat. . . ."

"There are more things to find out about in this house," the mongoose said to himself, "than all my family could find out in all their lives. I shall certainly stay and find out."

Questions

1. What do you think would happen if Teddy picked up the mongoose by its tail? Use information from the passage to support your answer. Write your answer on the lines below.

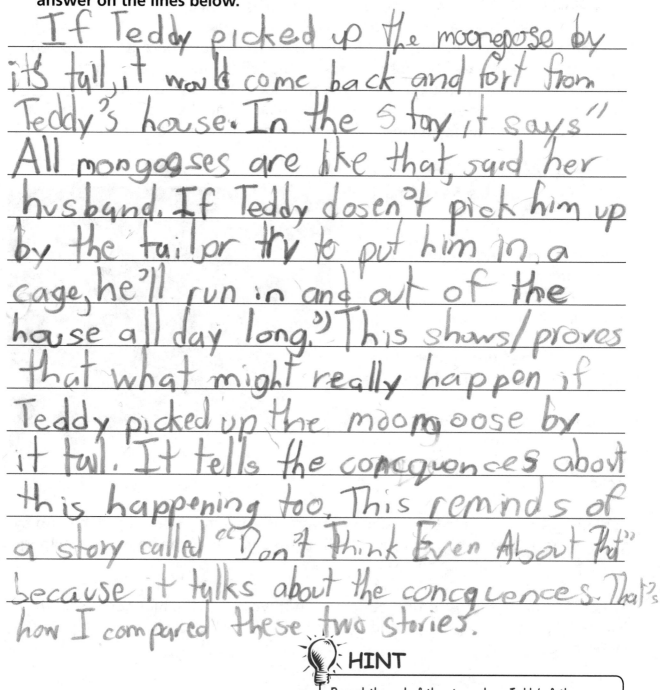

If Teddy picked up the moongoose by its tail, it would come back and fort from Teddy's house. In the story it says" All mongooses are like that, said her husband. If Teddy dosent pick him up by the tail or try to put him in a cage, he'll run in and out of the house all day long." This shows/proves that what might really happen if Teddy picked up the moongoose by it tail. It tells the concequences about this happening too. This reminds of a story called "Don't Think Even About That" because it tylks about the concequences. That's how I compared these two stories.

HINT

Reread the end of the story where Teddy's father says not to pick up the mongoose by its tail.

2. **Why did the author write this story?**

    (A) to show readers that a mongoose is nice

    (B) to teach readers about mongooses

    (C) to tell readers a story about a mongoose

    (D) to describe what a mongoose is like

 **HINT**

Do you think this story is real life or make-believe?
Remember that make-believe stories are written to
entertain.

3. **What do you think will happen next in the story? Write your answer on the lines below.**

_____

_____

_____

_____

_____

_____

_____

 **HINT**

Reread the last paragraph again. What do you think the
mongoose plans to do?

Passage 3

Read the passage below. Then answer the questions about the passage. Use the hints underneath each question to help you choose the right answer.

Rooms of Water

Many people keep fish in their homes. Some people have just one or two small fish. These fish might live in a goldfish bowl. People with larger fish, or many fish, might keep a fish tank. Maybe you even have one at your home or school. But chances are you couldn't fit Adventure Aquarium in your house.

Adventure Aquarium is in Camden, New Jersey. An aquarium is a large building full of fish tanks. Some of these tanks are *huge*. They need to be huge if they are going to hold all kinds of big fish and other water animals. People come from all around to see the swimming things that live at the aquarium.

You can find many kinds of animals at the aquarium. There are scary sharks, those big, smooth fish with sharp teeth. There are silly-looking seals, which look like big dogs with no hair and flippers for paws. You can see eels that look like huge swimming worms. You can see water animals of every size and shape. Some look like stars, some look like tiny horses, and some look like spiders. Some look like bats that play in the sand. Some animals are so strange you won't even know *what* they look like!

Some people go to the aquarium just to look at the many animals there. But the aquarium also offers a lot more than that. Almost every day, visitors can see special shows and events.

At the Jules Verne Gallery, you can see many animals from the deepest oceans. Jules Verne was a writer who imagined stories of people exploring the oceans. In Verne's stories, people found all sorts of wonderful animals and scary monsters in the ocean. Some of his stories have come true! In the aquarium, you can see real-life animals that Verne would have loved to meet.

Not everything that lives near the water is a fish. Not everything at the aquarium is a fish, either. One special kind of bird, the penguin, lives near water. Penguins can't fly, but they can walk and swim. They are black and white, and some people think they are funny-looking.

In some rooms at the aquarium, you can actually reach out and touch water animals. Some small animals are kept in pools in the Meet-a-Creature room. Visitors can stop at each pool and touch the animals. You may be surprised by the feel of these animals on your fingers. Some feel smooth like silk. Others are slimy and sticky. Still others are dry and bumpy.

You may even get the chance to touch a shark. One room has a shark pool. Visitors can reach in and pet the fish. Don't be worried, though. Sharks can be a danger in the wild. But in the aquarium, they won't hurt you.

If all that isn't enough for you, you may be able to get in the water yourself! A few lucky visitors are able to jump into a special pool. There, they can swim with sharks, seals, fish, and other great animals.

Aquariums are all about the water and the amazing animals that live in it. If you like fish, you might want to plan a trip to an aquarium soon.

Questions

1. **Why did the author write this passage?**

   Ⓐ to tell readers how to get to the aquarium

   Ⓑ to tell readers about sharks at the aquarium

   Ⓒ to inform readers about a great aquarium

   Ⓓ to entertain readers with a story about an aquarium

HINT

Cross off answer choices that you know are incorrect. Choose the answer choice that tells why the author wrote the whole passage.

2. **A small ocean animal that likes to be held by people would probably go in the**

   Ⓐ Jules Verne Gallery.

   Ⓑ shark tank.

   Ⓒ penguin room.

   Ⓓ Meet-a-Creature room.

HINT

Reread what kind of fish and animals are in each of these rooms. Then make your prediction.

3. **If you went to the Adventure Aquarium, what would you go to see first? Write your answer on the lines below.**

If I went to the Adventure Aquarium, I would see the penguins first because ~~fon~~ to me, they look so ~~so~~ cute. They look so adorable with their skin fins. I like how the penguins slitter through the water and how they wobble from side to side. I like that it swims so fast. ~~because one day,~~ They swim like this. "Whooooosh! Whooooosh!" Penguins are ~~er~~ really good dancers just like me. They like dancing just like I adore dancing around and around.

 **HINT**

Reread the passage. Choose what interests you most. Then explain why.

Chapter 5

Conclusions and Opinions

Clusters

A3 Forming of Opinions These questions elicit students' response to aspects of the text. The questions introduce a focus (for example, whether the main character would make a good friend) and ask students to select and analyze ideas and information from the text to develop a response. Given the nature of this task, these questions are always open-ended items.

A4 Making Judgments, Drawing Conclusions These questions ask students to draw conclusions based on knowledge they have garnered from the ideas and information within the text. For example, students might be asked to analyze how the setting (such as the season of the year) affects the sequence of events within a story, or to analyze the effect of skipping a step in a certain procedure.

Introduction

For some questions on the NJ ASK, you will have to draw a **conclusion**. A conclusion is a judgment. It's what you think based on what you have read. You won't find the answer to this kind of question in the passage. You will have to think about what you have read. Then you will have to choose the right answer. Sound hard? It might help to imagine that you are a detective. Detectives look for clues. Use the clues you find in the passage to help you answer the question.

In real life, you probably draw conclusions without even realizing it. Imagine that you see your friend crying. You would conclude that your friend is sad. Imagine that one of your new shoes is chewed to bits. You might conclude that your dog, Flea, chewed your shoe.

For other questions on this test, you will have to form an opinion. An **opinion** is what you think about something. Your opinion should be based on what you have read. It should make sense based on the details in the passage.

Practice Passage

Read this passage and answer the questions that follow.

Time with Dad

Greta spends time on the weekend with her dad. This time is special to her. One time, Dad taught Greta how to make spaghetti. Greta thinks her dad is a great cook! Another time, Greta and Dad went on a long walk. Today they are hanging pictures. Dad is teaching Greta how to use a hammer and nail. Greta likes this. She carefully holds the nail. Then she gently hammers the nail into the wall. Then Dad hangs a picture.

❔ Questions ❔

1. How does Greta feel about spending time with Dad?

Ⓐ She misses it.

Ⓑ She thinks it is just okay.

Ⓒ She would rather play.

Ⓓ She likes it a lot.

To answer this question, think about the details in the passage. One sentence in the passage says, "This time is special to her." The other details tell about the things Greta and Dad do together. Answer choice A says that Greta misses spending time with her dad. Does she miss him? She seems to be with him, so this is not a good answer. Answer choice B says that Greta "thinks it is just okay." She seems pretty excited about it, so this probably isn't the best answer. Answer choice C says that she would rather play. She seems to like being with her dad. It doesn't seem as if she would rather play. Answer choice D is a great answer. Greta likes spending time with her dad a lot!

2. What is the purpose of the nail?

Ⓐ It holds up the hammer.

Ⓑ It marks a spot on the wall.

Ⓒ It holds up the picture.

Ⓓ It makes a hole in the wall.

You have to use the details in the passage and your own experience to answer this question. The passage says that Greta holds the nail. Then she hammers the nail into the wall. Then Dad hangs a picture. The nail doesn't hold up the hammer. So answer choice A is not right. It might mark a spot on the wall. But this is not its main purpose. Answer choice B is not right either. The nail does hold up the picture. Choice C seems like the right answer. But always read all the answer choices! Choice D—the nail makes a hole in the wall—is true. But that isn't the nail's purpose. Answer choice C is best.

3. Would you like to do the things that Greta and Dad do together? Why or why not? Use information from the story to support your response. Write your answer on the lines below.

I don't like the things that Greta and Dad do togther because I don't like cooking or hanging up a picture. This is my opinion

Passage 1

Read the article below. Then answer the questions about the article. Use the hints underneath each question to help you choose the right answer.

Autumn's Amazing Leaves

It happens the same way every year. Long, hot summer days come to an end. Days get shorter and darkness falls sooner. It gets cooler outside. You trade your shorts and T-shirts for sweaters and jeans. It can only mean one thing.

Autumn is one of the most beautiful times of the year. It is at this time that the leaves on the trees begin to change colors. They are no longer the bright green of summer. Instead, they turn pretty shades of yellow, orange, red, brown, and even purple. But why exactly do leaves change their colors? Why don't they stay green all year?

It might seem strange, but the pretty colors that you see in autumn are found in leaves during the summer, too. You just can't see them. Something called chlorophyll, which gives leaves their green color, hides the other colors in the leaves.

You might not realize it, but during the spring and summer months, leaves are hard at work. They make the food that trees use to grow big and strong. Inside

green leaves, chlorophyll soaks in light from the sun. Just as you eat food so that you have energy, or power, to run around and play, leaves use sunlight for energy. This energy helps them turn gases and water in the air into food for the tree. Chlorophyll works very well when the days are long and hot. However, when the days get shorter and colder, chlorophyll starts to break down. It is then that the other colors in leaves begin to show.

Autumn leaves don't stick around for very long. After a few weeks of waving at you in the breeze, most of them are on the ground, instead of on trees. You might think that the wind blows the leaves down, and sometimes this is true. However, changes inside the tree can make the leaves fall off even without a breeze. As autumn continues, trees begin to close off the places where leaves are attached to branches. When these places are completely closed, the leaves are ready to fall.

It seems sad that beautiful fall leaves last for such a short time. But don't worry. Just because the leaves are no longer on trees does not mean they are being wasted. Once the leaves fall, they begin to dry out and break down. As this happens, the leaves fill the dirt on the ground with food that other plants need to grow.

The next time autumn rolls around, go out and enjoy the pretty colors on the trees. And remember, the leaves are not only pretty, but hard workers, too!

Questions

1. **How do most people feel about leaves in autumn?**

   Ⓐ They think the leaves are hard to see.

   Ⓑ They think green is better.

   ● They think the leaves are very pretty.

   Ⓓ They think the leaves will last a long time.

HINT

To answer this question, think about what the author says about the leaves. They turn many different colors. Do the leaves look nice? Do you think most people like this?

2. **Why do you think leaves stay green in places that are warm during the winter?**

    Ⓐ They get more sunlight.

    Ⓑ The trees grow wider and taller.

    Ⓒ The chlorophyll breaks down.

    Ⓓ They have only one color.

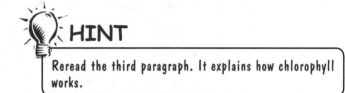

HINT

Reread the third paragraph. It explains how chlorophyll works.

3. **Do you think the leaves in autumn are beautiful? Why or why not? Use information from the article to support your answer. Write your answer on the lines below.**

I think the leaves are beautiful because the colors are different and they look very intresting.

HINT

This question asks for your opinion, but be sure to use details from the article in your answer.

Passage 2

Read the article below. Then answer the questions about the article. Use the hints underneath each question to help you choose the right answer.

The Best Game in the World

Have you ever heard of a game called Monopoly? You probably have. More people have played Monopoly than any other board game sold. *The Guinness Book of World Records* even wrote about the game. In fact, Monopoly is the best-selling board game all over the world!

In case you don't know, the point of the game is to be the player who ends up with the most money. The way to do this is to buy, rent, and sell land. As players make their way around the game board, they get the chance to buy one lot at a time as they land on the property. To be able to charge rent and build on the land, they need to put together a complete set of related properties. A complete property group is called a monopoly. In real life, whenever a person or company gains control in a given area over something worth money, they have a monopoly. For example, if you owned the only store in your town that sold ice cream, you would have a monopoly on ice cream.

In 1904, a woman named Lizzie Magie made up a board game called the Landlord's Game. The game was supposed to teach players about how a monopoly worked. This game changed over the years. When Magie moved to Chicago, she named each block on the game board after a street in Chicago. People fell in love with the game.

Somehow the game spread to Reading, Pennsylvania. There, a teacher used the game to teach his class about monopolies. Kids began to play the game with their friends after school. One young man moved back to his hometown of Indianapolis, Indiana, and remade the board game with his hometown's street names. He gave the game a new name and sold it to people there.

In Indianapolis a woman named Ruth Hoskins learned about the game and took a copy back to her hometown of Atlantic City, New Jersey. There, someone renamed all of the streets to match Atlantic City street names. The game spread to Philadelphia, Pennsylvania, where a man named Charles Darrow saw it. He, his wife, and his son started making Atlantic City game boards by hand and selling them.

The game sold so well that Darrow and his family could not make the games fast enough. Darrow teamed up with a friend who was a printer to make the game boards and cards. Darrow tried to sell the idea for his game to a company called Parker Brothers. They rejected Darrow's idea, because executives there felt it was not a good game. But Darrow improved his game, and Parker Brothers bought it. They even made a board on which the streets were named after streets in London, England. Parker Brothers sold that game all over Europe.

Parker Brothers still makes all kinds of different Monopoly games. They make Monopoly games with streets named after those in cities all over the world. However, how the game is played has not really changed since 1935. Most Americans play Monopoly on a board that uses Atlantic City street names, even though some of those streets and places are no longer around.

Questions

1. **How could you win a game of Monopoly?**

   Ⓐ by helping others buy land

   Ⓑ by giving money to a good cause

   Ⓒ by owning a lot of houses and hotels

   Ⓓ by selling things at a very low price

HINT

Reread the second paragraph of the article. How does a person win the game?

2. **What can you tell about most Monopoly games today?**

   Ⓐ They have Atlantic City street names.

   Ⓑ They are sold in Chicago.

   Ⓒ They are played by grown-ups.

   Ⓓ They have different game rules.

HINT

Reread the end of the article. What can you tell is true of most Monopoly games in the United States?

3. **Would you like to play Monopoly? Why or why not? Use information from the article to support your answer. Write your answer on the lines below.**

_____

_____

_____

_____

_____

_____

_____

_____

_____

_____

_____

_____

_____

_____

Passage 3

Read the article below. Then answer the questions about the article. Use the hints underneath each question to help you choose the right answer.

Beatrix Potter

Beatrix Potter is best known as a writer of stories for children. She wrote about the famous character Peter Rabbit. But she was so much more than just a writer.

Beatrix was born in London, England, in 1866. She spent a lot of time at home, because her parents didn't want her to go to school. Instead, they hired teachers to come to their house and teach Beatrix music and art. Beatrix and her younger brother Bertram were best friends and spent a lot of time together.

In the summer, the Potter family often visited a place in England called the Lake District. Here, Beatrix and Bertram learned to love nature. They spent hours in the woods, catching and studying different animals. Both Potter children were very good at drawing. Beatrix loved drawing pictures of the animals, plants, and flowers.

Beatrix and Bertram had pet rabbits, lizards, frogs, snakes, mice—Beatrix even had a hedgehog named Mrs. Tiggy-winkle and a pig named Pig-Wig! Beatrix and her brother had a lot of fun with their animals. One rabbit, Benjamin Bouncer, loved to eat hot toast with butter, and another, Peter Piper, learned how to jump through a hoop. Many of these animals later showed up in Beatrix's stories.

Beatrix continued to draw animals into her adulthood. When she was 24, she sold some rabbit drawings to a greeting card company. Her first book of drawings was printed in 1890.

One of Beatrix's favorite things to do was send letters to children she knew. She liked to draw pictures in the letters to make the children happy. In 1893, Beatrix wrote a letter to Noel Moore, a five-year-old who was sick in bed. Beatrix wrote a story to amuse him. She made up a story about four rabbits named Flopsy, Mopsy, Cottontail, and Peter. She drew pictures for Noel on the letter. Noel loved the letter so much that Beatrix decided to make a Peter Rabbit book. She called it *The Tale of Peter Rabbit*. Beatrix took her book to different book-printing companies called publishers. None of the publishers wanted Beatrix's book.

Finally, in 1902, Beatrix's book was published. Children all over England loved her story. Over the next 28 years, Beatrix would publish 22 more books. They were all stories about animals. She did all of the drawings for her books. Children loved the drawings, especially in some of her more famous books, like *The Tale of Squirrel Nutkin*, *The Tale of Benjamin Bunny*, *The Tale of Mrs. Tiggy-Winkle*, *The Tale of Tom Kitten*, *The Tale of Jemima Puddle Duck*, and *The Tale of the Flopsy Bunnies*.

After making some money on *The Tale of Peter Rabbit*, Beatrix was able to buy some land in the Lake District area, where she had spent so much time as a child. She bought a farm and began a new life as a farmer. She worked right in the fields with the men. Whenever Beatrix made money on her books, she bought a little more land. During this time, Beatrix met a man named William Heelis, who also loved the Lake District. The two were married in 1913.

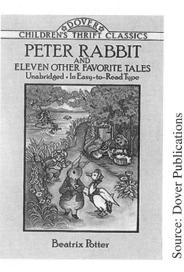

Source: Dover Publications

Beatrix and William settled into farming together. They raised rare, prize-winning sheep, and they kept rabbits and other farm animals to please the children who came to visit them. They continued to buy land in the Lake District. Nearby farmers were happy that Beatrix and William were buying land. They knew that Beatrix was part of the National Trust, a group of people who protected land by buying it. When Beatrix died in 1943, she left 4,000 acres of land to the National Trust, including 15 farms. Because of Beatrix, this land is still protected and looks just as beautiful as it did when she bought it. Thousands of people visit it each year to see the natural beauty that Beatrix cared for and loved so much.

 Questions

1. **What can you tell about Beatrix from the article?**

    Ⓐ She liked being with children.

    Ⓑ She liked going to school.

    Ⓒ She fought often with her brother.

    Ⓓ She always wanted to be a farmer.

 HINT

Think about the main reason Beatrix wrote her books. Who were her books for?

2. Explain how the animals Beatrix kept as a child gave her ideas for her books. Use information from the article to support your answer. Write your answer on the lines below.

_____

_____

_____

_____

_____

_____

_____

_____

_____

_____

_____

_____

_____

_____

HINT

Reread the fourth paragraph of the article.

3. **Do you think you would like to read Beatrix's books? Why or why not? Use information from the article to support your answer. Write your answer on the lines below.**

I think I would like to read Beatrix's books because I adore reading stories for children. In the story it says "Beatrix Potter is best known as a writer of stories for children." This statment proves the reason why I think I would like to read Beatrix's books. This piece of text reminds me of another passage I read called "Read Cookie's book" because that story has a writer named Cookie and tells why people should read that story. This is how that story is simmilar to this piece of text if I compared this two storys.

HINT

Read through the article again. Look for details about Beatrix's books. Think about whether you would like to read a book like this.

Chapter 6

Made-Up Stories

Clusters

A5 Literary Elements and Textual Conventions NJ ASK questions on these subjects focus on devices used by the author. Students might be asked to analyze what a specific metaphor conveys about a character in the story, or why an author uses italics for certain words.

W5 Recognition of Text Organization Text organization encompasses the patterns of organization that characterize the respective genres. For the narratives, questions focus on setting, character, and plot, as well as on any distinctive pattern within the story, such as repetition.

Introduction

Some questions on the test ask you about made-up stories and poems. Made-up stories have some things in common. They have a setting. They also have characters and a plot. Poems also have some of these things.

Authors think a lot about the stories they write. They do a lot of planning. When they do something special, like put a word in *italics*, it's for a reason. In this chapter, you'll learn more about made-up stories and poems.

Setting

A short story or poem takes place somewhere. Where and when a story takes place is called the **setting**. A poem can also have a setting. Read this paragraph.

Melissa was burying her toes in the sand. She could hear a seagull cry out in the distance. It was a beautiful day. Then a wave crashed into Melissa. She laughed. The cool water hitting her skin made her jump and run.

Where does this story take place? If you guessed the beach, you're right!

Characters

Stories have characters. Characters may be people. But they may also be animals or things. Characters say and do things in the story. The character that says and does the most is called the main character. A story may have more than one main character.

Read this very short story.

Learning to Fly

Little Robin sat on a branch next to her mother. "Go ahead now. Flap your wings," said Mother Robin. Little Robin was afraid. She didn't want to fly. But she did as she was told. She flapped her wings a little. "Flap them harder than that," said Mother Robin. Little Robin flapped her wings harder. Before she knew it, she was in the air! She flapped her wings gently until she had flown from the tree to the ground.

Write the names of the two characters in this story on the lines below.

Little Robin and Mother Robin are the two characters in this Story as shown below.

Plot

What happens in a story is called the **plot**. It includes the main events in a story. These events move the story from the beginning to the end. In most stories, the characters have a problem. This problem is part of the plot. How the characters deal with the problem is also part of the plot.

In the story "Learning to Fly," Little Robin's problem is that she is afraid to fly. She solves her problem by listening to her mother. These are the major events in the story:

1. Little Robin's mother tells her to flap her wings.
2. Little Robin flaps her wings.
3. Little Robin's mother tells her to flap her wings harder.
4. Little Robin flaps her wings harder.
5. Little Robin is in the air and flies to the ground.

Special Language and Type

Sometimes authors use special language in their stories and poems. Sometimes they use special type, such as all CAPITAL letters, or *italics* and **boldface** lettering. Read the paragraph below:

> Lilly pedaled her bike up the big hill. It was very hot outside. She really wanted to go home and have something cool to drink. If she could just get up this hill. . . . Just then Lily felt her feet pushing on the pedals too quickly. She knew it. Her bike chain had come off AGAIN. "Ah, my friend," Lilly said, and looked at her broken bike. "You have failed me big-time."

❓ Questions ❓

1. **Why do you think the author put the word "AGAIN" in all capital letters?**

I think the author put the word "AGAIN" in all capital letters because something happened so many times.

2. **Why does Lilly call her bike "my friend"?**

_____

_____

Passage 1

Read the story below. Then answer the questions about the story. Use the hints underneath each question to help you choose the right answer.

Ali's Kitten

As the sun started to dip behind the top of the mountain, Ali lay in the grass in her front yard, staring straight up at the clouds that swam slowly across the sky. As she turned her head, grass rubbed against her face and scratched her ear. Her dog, Nan, did not move, but Ali felt his breath on her leg. Winter was coming, and Ali did not like the cold. She smiled when she remembered the fun she had had all summer with Nan. Soon they would be unable to lie in the warm grass and enjoy the sun, so how would they spend their days?

Suddenly Nan jumped up and looked down the mountain where Ali could not see. She sat up quickly and followed his gaze toward a small animal coming toward them; it was a cat. Nan growled and Ali told him to be kind. "Nice Nan," she warned. The dog sat back on his legs but kept his eyes on the small cat, which Ali could now see was just a kitten. "Here, kitty," she called, but the cat held still. Nan always seemed to sense what Ali wanted. He lay down on the ground and rolled over on his back to show the cat that he was playful, not mean.

As the kitten began walking toward them again, Ali noticed its white fur was very dirty. The cat picked up speed until it was almost upon them. Then the kitten hopped onto Nan's belly, where it lay down, looked up at Ali, and meowed as if asking a question. Nan allowed the kitten to lie on his furry belly, and when Ali petted the kitten's soft fur, it purred, closed its eyes, and fell quickly to sleep.

What was this tiny kitten doing so high up on the mountain all alone? It needed a home. Ali thought about how the animal would get through the winter. As Ali wondered, Nan licked the kitten's fur clean. Since they lived on a farm and they had lots of room, Ali was pretty sure her mother would let her keep the kitten. Ali and Nan didn't have to worry about finding something to do during the cold winter days. Something had found them.

 Questions

1. **Who is the main character in this story?**

   Ⓐ Ali

   Ⓑ Nan

   Ⓒ a kitten

   Ⓓ Ali's mother

   HINT

   Be careful! The story is about a kitten, but the main character is the one who says and does the most in the story.

2. **What is Ali's problem in the beginning of the story?**

   Ⓐ She wonders whether Nan will be nice to the kitten.

   Ⓑ She wonders whether the kitten has a home.

   Ⓒ She wonders what she will do in the winter.

   Ⓓ She wonders whether she can keep the kitten.

   HINT

   Reread the beginning of the story. What is Ali worried about?

3. **When does most of this story take place?**

   Ⓐ in the spring

   Ⓑ in the summer

   Ⓒ in the fall

   Ⓓ in the winter

   HINT

   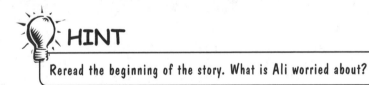

   Remember that Ali is lying in the grass in the warm sun, but she says that winter is coming.

Passage 2

Read the story below. Then answer the questions about the story. Use the hints underneath each question to help you choose the right answer.

When I Grow Up

Mrs. Dixon, the third-grade teacher, stood at the front of the room and smiled at her class. Kyle liked her smile. Mrs. Dixon was really nice, and she was a great teacher, too. "Class, I have an exciting project for you to work on this week."

Kyle smiled. He liked working on projects, especially exciting ones.

Mrs. Dixon continued. "I want you to think about what you would like to be when you grow up. Then I'd like you to write an essay telling everyone why you would like to do this special job. I'd like you to put your essay on a poster and decorate the poster with pictures of people doing this job. We're going to hang the posters around the classroom so it will look really great on Parents' Night."

Kyle frowned. This was not good. He had no idea what he wanted to be when he grew up. During lunch, he talked to his friends about the project. Rubina knew that she wanted to be a doctor when she grew up. She really wanted to help people. Emile knew that he wanted to work with computers. Jonathan knew that he wanted to be a firefighter. Chrissy wanted to be a veterinarian so she could spend her days working with animals. Kyle was the only one who did not know what he wanted to be.

"What do you like to do?" Rubina asked, trying to help him.

"Nothing, really. All I really like to do is read books."

"Well, that's something! Maybe you'd like to be a writer," Chrissy said.

Kyle shook his head. "I don't like to write stories. I really just like to read them.

"Do you like being outdoors?" Emile asked. "Maybe you could be a forest ranger!"

"No," Kyle said. "I don't like being in the sun. And I really don't like bugs."

"Maybe you could be a teacher," Rubina offered.

"No, I think I'm too shy. And all that talking would make me really tired."

After lunch, Mrs. Dixon gave the class some time to start writing their essays. Kyle was starting to worry. What was he going to do? What would happen if he couldn't think of anything? What would his parents say when he didn't have an essay and a poster on Parents' Night?

Kyle decided to ask Mrs. Dixon for help. "Mrs. Dixon, I have a really, really big problem. I don't know what I would like to be when I grow up. Really, I don't have a clue."

Mrs. Dixon told him to sit in the chair next to her desk so they could spend some time talking. "What do your parents do for a living?" Mrs. Dixon asked.

"My father is a nurse and my mother works at a business," Kyle said.

"Would you like be a nurse, or work at a business?"

"No, not really."

"What do you like to do when you're not in school?" asked Mrs. Dixon.

"I like to read," Kyle said.

"Would you like to be a writer?"

Kyle rolled his eyes. "No, I really just like to read."

"Kyle, where do you like to go when you're not in school?"

Kyle told Mrs. Dixon that he spent a lot of time at the library on his block. He spent so much time there, in fact, that he knew the librarians by name. One of them, Mrs. Hemsley, even set aside books that she thought Kyle would like to read.

Mrs. Dixon raised her eyebrows. "Kyle," she said, "did you ever think that maybe you would like to work in the library someday? Maybe you would like to be a librarian."

Kyle smiled. "I think I might like to do that," he said. "I would definitely like to spend all day in a library. Thanks, Mrs. Dixon!"

Kyle went back to his seat. He couldn't wait to start writing his essay. He was going to be a librarian when he grew up. Maybe he would even get to work in the library in his neighborhood. Kyle started to write his essay. This project was *really* exciting, and he was going to do a great job!

Questions

1. **Where does most of this story take place?**

   Ⓐ in a library

   Ⓑ in a classroom

   Ⓒ in a business

   Ⓓ in a lunchroom

 **HINT**

This question asks about the setting of the story. Kyle and his friends are in a lunchroom for only a little while, and Kyle and Mrs. Dixon talk about the library, but most of the story does not take place in these places.

2. **Who is the main character in this story?**

   Ⓐ Mrs. Dixon

   Ⓑ Kyle

   Ⓒ Emile

   Ⓓ Rubina

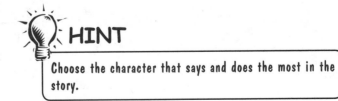 **HINT**

Choose the character that says and does the most in the story.

3. **What is Kyle's problem in the story?**

Ⓐ He does not want to write an essay.

Ⓑ He does not want to go to Parents' Night.

Ⓒ He does not know what he wants to be.

Ⓓ He does not like being outdoors in the sun.

HINT

Think about why Kyle was upset when Mrs. Dixon asked the students to write about what they would like to be when they grow up.

4. **How does Kyle solve his problem? Write your answer on the lines below.**

3/4

Kyle solves his problem by getting help from Mrs. Dixon. Mrs. Dixon gives him books to read. He liked those books. and knew what to write in his essay. He waited to be ~~write~~ a librarian because he likes books. That's how Kyle solves his problem.

HINT

How does Mrs. Dixon help Kyle?

Mrs. Dixon advised Kyle to become a librarian when he grows up because he is fond of books.

Passage 3

Read the story below. Then answer the questions about the story. Use the hints underneath each question to help you choose the right answer.

The Emperor and the Nightingale

adapted from a classic fairy tale

Once upon a time there was an emperor who lived in a huge palace. He filled his palace with many beautiful things. People from all over the world came to see his palace and all of his things. They were so happy to be there that they didn't want to leave. "Oh, please, dear emperor, show us just one more beautiful thing," they pleaded. But the emperor did not have any more beautiful things.

A fisherman overheard their cries. He approached the visitors outside the palace. "I can show you one more beautiful thing," he said. "I can show you the most beautiful thing in all of China." The people wanted to see the most beautiful thing in all of China. So they followed the fisherman deep into the forest. There he showed them a little gray bird.

"You made us walk all this way to see a plain little bird?" asked one of the visitors. "It's not beautiful!" Then the little bird, a nightingale, opened its beak and began to sing. It was the most beautiful song any of the people had ever heard. It was, indeed, the most beautiful thing in all of China.

When the visitors returned home, they told all of their friends about the nightingale. More people came to see the nightingale.

Soon everyone in China knew about the nightingale. Everyone except the emperor, that is, and the people who worked for him in his palace. The emperor was very old and rarely left the palace. He had never seen the nightingale or heard its song.

Then one day the emperor of China received a letter from the emperor of Japan. "I have heard many people talk of your beautiful nightingale," wrote the emperor of Japan. "I will arrive at your palace in two days. I would like to see you and your beautiful bird."

The emperor of China was confused. What beautiful bird? He called one of his guards. "Are nightingales beautiful?" the emperor asked.

"No, they are not," replied the guard. "In fact, they are quite plain."

"Well, the emperor of Japan will be here in two days and expects to see this nightingale."

Then the emperor ordered the guard to find the nightingale and bring it back to him.

The guard searched the palace. He looked carefully in each room. He searched the attic and the basement, but he could not find the nightingale. The guard searched the palace gardens and around the ponds. He could not find the nightingale.

Then it was the morning on which the emperor of Japan would arrive. The guard kept on looking for the nightingale. He was just about to give up when the fisherman took him into the forest and showed him the nightingale.

They brought the nightingale back to the palace just in time. The emperor of Japan had arrived. "So this is the famous nightingale," he said. "It doesn't look beautiful at all." Then the little bird flew to the windowsill and opened its beak and began to sing. Its song was so beautiful that all of the people in the room cried.

"Thank you, my friend," said the emperor of Japan, "for letting me hear the most beautiful song in the world."

Later, the emperor of China gave the nightingale a golden perch to sit on. Each time the bird sang his beautiful song, the emperor cried tears of joy. But many of the people in the palace said they wished that the nightingale looked as pretty as he sounded. This made the emperor angry. He did not like people saying bad things about the bird that brought him so much happiness.

So he tried to make the nightingale look better. He put a gold crown on his head and wrapped some colorful ribbons around his body. Now the nightingale looked nice, but was only allowed to fly out of its cage two times a day. Lots of people came to see the nightingale, and it sang for them. The emperor noticed that the nightingale looked sad and tired.

Each night the emperor invited the nightingale into his bedroom. The emperor told the nightingale stories about what life was like when he was a boy. The nightingale listened to the emperor and then sang him a special song. "You don't need a golden perch or crown or colorful ribbons," the emperor said. "You are the most beautiful thing in the whole world."

Soon the emperor of Japan sent the emperor of China a toy nightingale. It was covered in jewels and made of gold. On its back was a small golden key. When the emperor turned the key, the bird sang one of the real nightingale's songs. The song was not as lovely as the ones the real nightingale sang, and it could only sing the same song over and over. But no one seemed to care.

The people of the palace loved the toy nightingale. "Finally, a bird that looks as lovely as it sounds," they said. The people ignored the real nightingale, so it flew back to its home in the forest.

No one missed the real nightingale except for the emperor. He missed his friend very much. But he thought that it was probably for the best. The nightingale seemed sad and tired in its cage and was probably happier in the forest.

The people never tired of listening to the toy bird sing. They played its song over and over until one day—pop!—one of its springs broke and it stopped singing. A toy maker fixed it, but said that they could only wind the key once in a while.

The emperor was very sad. He had lost his best friend, the real nightingale, and now he didn't even have the toy nightingale. In time, he grew sick and weak. When the fisherman learned that the emperor was sick, he went to find the real nightingale.

The real nightingale flew into the emperor's bedroom, perched on his bed, and sang his beautiful song. "You're back!" the emperor exclaimed. "My beautiful nightingale has returned!" Each day, the nightingale flew out of the emperor's window and returned to the forest. Then, at night, the nightingale flew into the emperor's bedroom and perched on his bed. Within a few days, color returned to the emperor's cheeks and he began to feel better.

"This is all because of you, my friend," the emperor told the nightingale. This made the nightingale very happy. He loved the emperor, because he was the one person who did not want to change him. The emperor loved the nightingale even if his feathers were plain gray.

 Questions

1. **Where does most of the story take place?**

    Ⓐ in a palace

    Ⓑ in a bedroom

    Ⓒ in a forest

    Ⓓ in a garden

    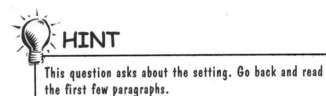HINT

    This question asks about the setting. Go back and read the first few paragraphs.

2. **What problem do people have with the real nightingale?**

    Ⓐ They don't like his singing.

    Ⓑ His spring is broken.

    Ⓒ He can sing only one song.

    Ⓓ They don't like his color.

    HINT

    Remember why the nightingale flies away. And think about what people like about the toy nightingale.

3. Why does the author use an exclamation point in the sentence that follows: "The people never tired of listening to the toy bird sing. They played its song over and over until one day—pop!—one of its springs broke and it stopped singing"?

    Ⓐ to show that many people heard the pop

    Ⓑ to show that people liked the bird

    Ⓒ to show that the pop was loud

    Ⓓ to show that the bird was not real

 HINT

Think about the sound a spring might make when it pops. Also think about why an author would use an exclamation point.

4. Where does the end of the story take place?

    Ⓐ in the palace garden

    Ⓑ in the fisherman's house

    Ⓒ in the emperor's bedroom

    Ⓓ in the nightingale's forest

 HINT

Reread the end of the story if you're not sure of this answer. Where are the emperor and the nightingale?

Chapter 7

Prewriting

What Is Prewriting?

Good writers do some work before they begin writing. **Prewriting** is a process that helps writers plan what they will write about. It is the way that good writers form clear ideas for their writing. It helps them figure out what they want to say in their writing.

When prewriting, you should think about who will read your writing, or your **audience**. You should also think about why you are writing, or the **purpose** of your writing.

Writing on the NJ ASK

On the NJ ASK, you are asked to complete two different writing tasks. To do this, you must read writing prompts. A **writing prompt** is a set of directions for your writing. A writing prompt might be a question that you have to answer, or it might be a set of instructions. A writing prompt gives you a topic to write about. It makes you think about a certain subject and then what you might want to write about that subject.

The NJ ASK test booklet includes blank pages where you **prewrite**, or plan your writing. You won't receive any score for what you write on these blank pages. The blank pages are followed by pages of lines. This is where you write the final draft of your writing. The final draft of your writing is scored.

This lesson teaches you what kinds of prompts you will see on the test. It also teaches you how to prewrite in response to a writing prompt. There are two writing prompts on the NJ ASK.

Expository Prompt

The **expository prompt** has two formats. One gives a short verbal prompt and directs you to write a composition about that topic. The second expository prompt will be preceded by a poem. You won't be asked to write about the poem. The poem will simply introduce a specific subject. You will write a composition about that subject.

You will have 30 minutes to respond to each writing prompt. You should use the first few minutes to prewrite, or make a written plan of what you will write about. You should use the last few minutes to look over your answer and make any changes that you think will make your writing better. You can use a tool called a writer's checklist to help you make sure that your writing is good. You will see a writer's checklist later in this lesson.

Parts of a Writing Prompt

Each writing prompt has the following parts:

- An important topic that gets you to think
- A clear focus

- A clear theme or central idea

- A clear purpose

- A background situation, or context, that helps you think about the topic

To get a good score on the writing section of the test, your writing should do the following:

- Reflect your age and grade level.

- Have a clear focus with a clear purpose, or reason that you are writing.

- Be supported by details that make sense.

- Be clearly organized, with a clear opening and closing.

- Use different types of words and different kinds of sentences.

- Have a strong stance, or reflect a clear opinion or point of view.

- Show that you understand how to write for a certain audience.

Think about these things as you begin to write. Knowing what is expected of your writing before you begin gives you a better idea of what to write.

Ways to Prewrite

Your prewriting doesn't have to be perfect. You don't have to use complete sentences. You don't have to have clear ideas. You just need to put some ideas on paper. Then you can look at them and decide which ones you will use in your writing. You can do this by making a list, making a web, or using another kind of graphic organizer. You will learn how to do this in the prompt practice sections of this lesson.

How to Prewrite for a Expository Prompt

On the NJ ASK, you are given a prompt. Then you are asked to write a story about what might be happening next in that story. You are also given a writer's checklist. The writer's checklist on the NJ ASK helps you make sure that you stay on track while you write. It tells you which parts of your writing you should improve to get a better score.

Here is an example of the writer's checklist on the NJ ASK test. The boldface sentences have to do especially with prewriting.

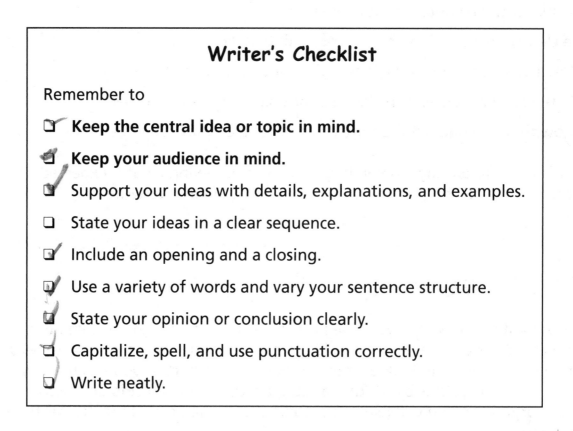

Writer's Checklist

Remember to

☑ **Keep the central idea or topic in mind.**

☑ **Keep your audience in mind.**

☑ Support your ideas with details, explanations, and examples.

❑ State your ideas in a clear sequence.

☑ Include an opening and a closing.

☑ Use a variety of words and vary your sentence structure.

☑ State your opinion or conclusion clearly.

☑ Capitalize, spell, and use punctuation correctly.

❑ Write neatly.

Sample Writing Task

An expository prompt on the NJ ASK looks something like this:

> **Read the following prompt:**
>
> **Mike and Anna had planned this day for a long time. This last week had seemed as if it would last forever!**
>
> **Write a story about what Mike and Anna did for their special day.**
>
> **You may take notes, create a web, or do other prewriting work in the space provided on the following pages. Then write your story on the pages that contain lines.**

● ● ●

You have seen what the expository prompt can look like. Now take another look at the prompt. What do you think might be happening next? What details should you think about to help yourself form a story? These are the questions you need to answer in your prewriting space.

To begin prewriting, you might want to make a list. When you are trying to come up with a story about this prompt, you could make a list of questions and then answer those questions. Your might want to make your list on a hand like this:

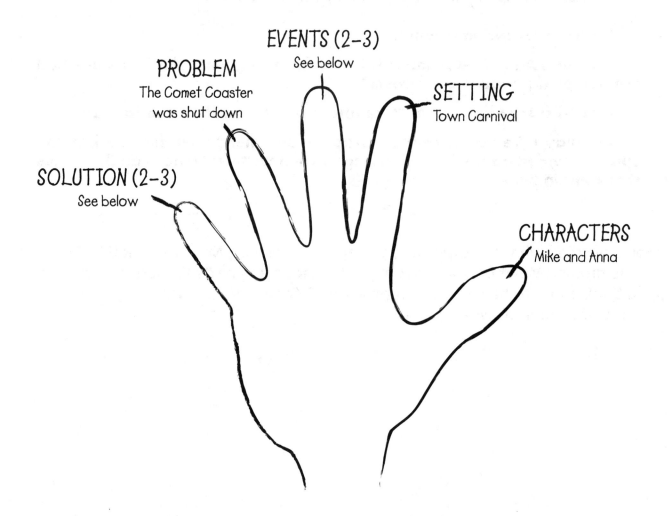

EVENTS (2–3)
See below

PROBLEM
The Comet Coaster
was shut down

SETTING
Town Carnival

SOLUTION (2–3)
See below

CHARACTERS
Mike and Anna

EVENTS LEADING TO PROBLEM

1. They ran over to the town carnival.

2. They got their ride tickets.

3. They ran over to their favorite ride the "Comet Coaster."

PROBLEM: Their favorite ride was shut down.

EVENTS TO SOLVE THE PROBLEM (try to have at least 2 or 3)

1. They ran over to the ride and asked the man how long it would be shut down. The man said an hour.

2. Mike and Anna decided not to waste their time so they got cotton candy and they walked around.

3. When they came back in an hour the Comet Coaster was working again.

CONCLUSION

They had a great day riding the Comet Coaster after all.

You can make up any story that comes to your mind. You don't know what Mike and Anna had planned, but you have given them a story. You have prewritten a handful of ideas about the prompt. Now you can write a story about the prompt. This is what you will do on the NJ ASK.

You can also pre-write using any kind of graphic organizers. You can put your notes about the prompt into a graphic organizer that looks like this:

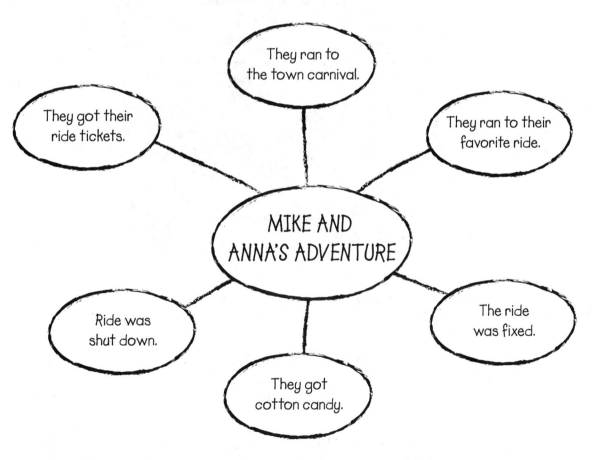

These are just a couple of ways to prewrite. When you practice prewriting yourself then you will figure out which way works best for you.

How to Prewrite for an Expository Prompt that Includes a Poem Prompt

On the NJ ASK, you will be asked to read a poem. Then you will be asked to write a composition based on an idea in the poem. You are also given a writer's checklist to help you write a good composition about that idea.

A poem prompt on the NJ ASK looks like this:

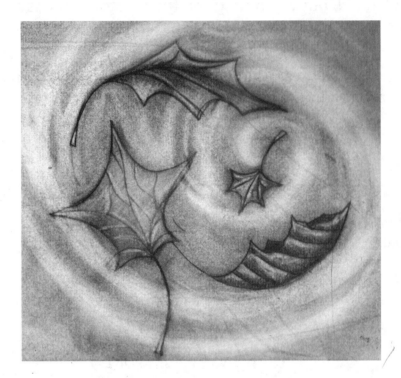

Sample Writing Task

An Autumn Greeting

Anonymous

"Come," said the Wind to the Leaves one day.
"Come over to the meadow and we will play.
Put on your dresses of red and gold.
For summer is gone and the days grow cold."

In "An Autumn Greeting," the poet writes about the leaves changing colors in the fall. In many states, the changing leaves signal the changing of the seasons from summer to fall. At one time or another, you have probably noticed some other signs that fall has arrived. Write a composition about other ways you can tell the seasons have changed from summer to fall.

In your composition, be sure to do the following:

- **Describe at least two signs of fall.**

- **Explain how you can notice these signs.**

- **Tell how these signs make you feel about the changing of the season.**

You may take notes, create a web, or do other prewriting work on the blank pages provided. Then write your composition on the pages with lines.

● ● ●

That is what the poem prompt looks like. Think about the things you notice when the season changes from summer to fall. Then start prewriting. If you choose to write a list, it may look something like this:

Signs of fall:

- The air starts to smell different.
- Kids go back to school.
- Stores have back-to-school sales.
- You start to want hot drinks like tea and apple cider.
- You start to wear jackets and sweaters at night.
- The air seems crisp and clean, not hazy and humid.

Now choose the best ideas on your list to write about. What ideas will be most interesting to your audience? Which ideas can you write the most detail about? Which things about the changing seasons do you like? Which don't you like? Which do you want to write about?

Creating a graphic organizer like the one below can help you when you are ready to write your essay.

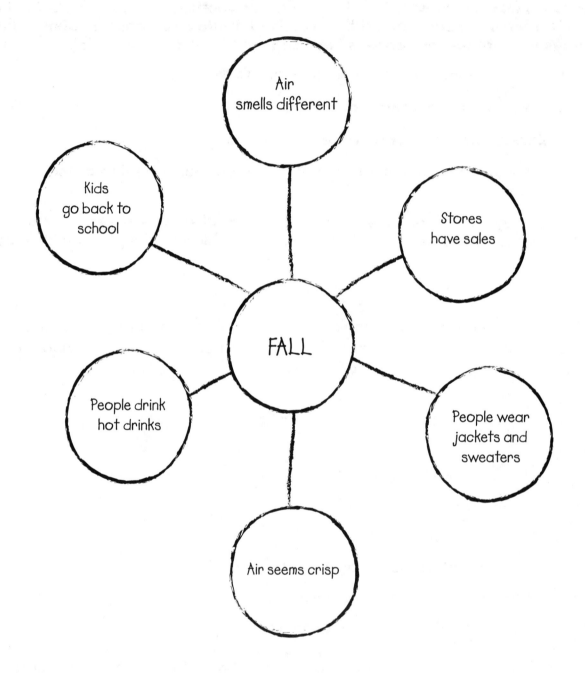

Another way to pre-write your composition is to break up your ideas into three paragraphs.

Paragraph 1

State your topic or problem. Describe that topic or problem in detail. Build background: Who is involved with you, where/when does the event take place?

Paragraph 2

Name and explain 3 details of the topic or problem.

Paragraph 3

Restate your topic. Tell how the topic ended or how the problem was solved.

In the next chapter of this book, you will learn how to begin writing your essay.

Chapter 8

Drafting and Revising

Drafting

In the previous chapter, you learned about prewriting. You learned that doing some prewriting will help you when you begin to write. In this chapter, you will learn how to draft your essay. When you draft your essay, you begin writing it.

Remember the writer's checklist you read in the last chapter? It's printed again below. But this time, the sentences that are boldface have to do with drafting.

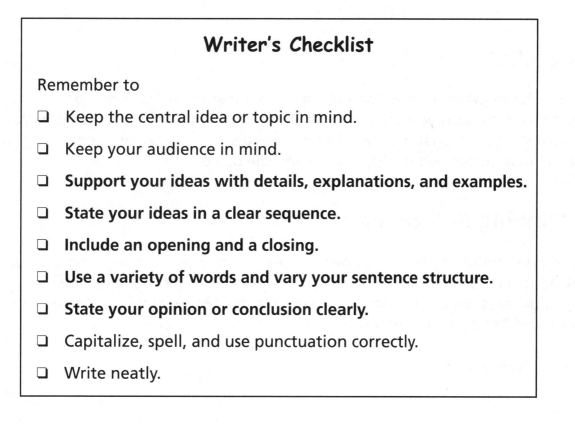

Writer's Checklist

Remember to

❑ Keep the central idea or topic in mind.

❑ Keep your audience in mind.

❑ **Support your ideas with details, explanations, and examples.**

❑ **State your ideas in a clear sequence.**

❑ **Include an opening and a closing.**

❑ **Use a variety of words and vary your sentence structure.**

❑ **State your opinion or conclusion clearly.**

❑ Capitalize, spell, and use punctuation correctly.

❑ Write neatly.

Details

When you write your essay, make sure you include enough details to make your point. A detail can be anything that supports your main idea. It can be an example. It can be an explanation. If you were writing in response to the poem prompt in the last chapter, you would need details to help the reader to know about the signs of fall. If you don't include details, your reader might not understand what is going on.

In the last chapter, we included some details about fall. Do you remember them? If not, we've included them here.

- The air starts to smell different.

- Kids go back to school.

- Stores have back-to-school sales.

- You start to want hot drinks like tea and apple cider.

- You start to wear jackets and sweaters at night.

- The air seems crisp and clean, not hazy and humid.

Sequence

The order of events is called **sequence**. Tell your story in sequence, or in an order that makes sense. If you are writing the story about Mike and Anna's day, you should start with what happened first. Then discuss what happened during the day. Finally, discuss what happened when the day ended.

Beginning and Ending

Your essay should have an **introduction**. An introduction is a beginning. Your introduction doesn't have to be fancy, but your essay should have one. An introduction should tell what your essay is about. For example, in the essay about Mike and Anna, you might write this:

The day had finally come!

This sentence tells what your story will be about. After this sentence, you can tell what happened during the day, and then what happened at the end of the day.

Word Variety

When you write, you should use a variety of words and sentences. The word "variety" simply means "different kinds." Read the sentences below:

A boy was named Tommy. Tommy learned about wishes. Tommy learned about this from his grandmother. Tommy liked this. Tommy liked learning about wishes.

Did you enjoy reading those sentences? No! They're very short. They also use the name "Tommy" too often.

Now read these sentences:

A boy named Tommy learned about wishes from his grandmother. Tommy liked learning about wishes.

Much better!

Opinions and Conclusions

An **opinion** is what you think about something. A **conclusion** is a judgment you make from details. For example, suppose you see your little sister with a big scratch on her hand. She is crying. You might conclude that she is sad because your cat, Pepper, scratched her. Your opinion about the situation might be that Pepper did a bad thing.

When you express your opinions or draw conclusions on the NJ ASK, include enough details to show the reader why you think the way that you do.

How to Write a Draft for a Prompt

Remember the expository prompt from the previous chapter? It's printed again here, along with the hand diagram and graphic organizer.

Sample Writing Task

A speculative prompt on the NJ ASK looks something like this:

Read the following prompt:

Mike and Anna had planned this day for a long time. This last week had seemed as if it would last forever!

Write a story about what Mike and Anna did for their special day.

You may take notes, create a web, or do other prewriting work in the space provided on the following pages. Then write your story on the pages that contain lines.

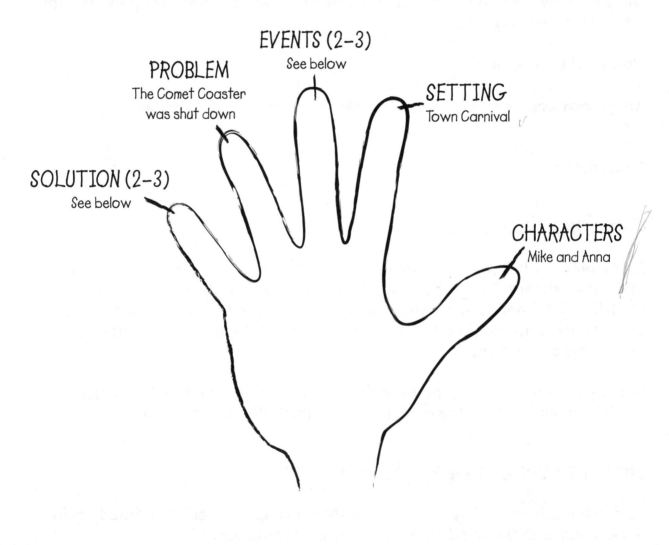

EVENTS (2–3)
See below

PROBLEM
The Comet Coaster
was shut down

SETTING
Town Carnival

SOLUTION (2–3)
See below

CHARACTERS
Mike and Anna

EVENTS LEADING TO PROBLEM

1. They ran over to the town carnival.

2. They got their ride tickets.

3. They run over to their favorite ride the "Comet Coaster."

PROBLEM: Their favorite ride was shut down.

EVENTS TO SOLVE THE PROBLEM (try to have at least 2 or 3)

1. They run over to the ride and ask the man how long it will be shut down for. The man said an hour.

2. Mike and Anna decided not to waste their time so they got cotton candy and they walked around.

3. When they came back in and hour the Comet Coaster was working again.

CONCLUSION

They had a great day riding the Comet Coaster after all.

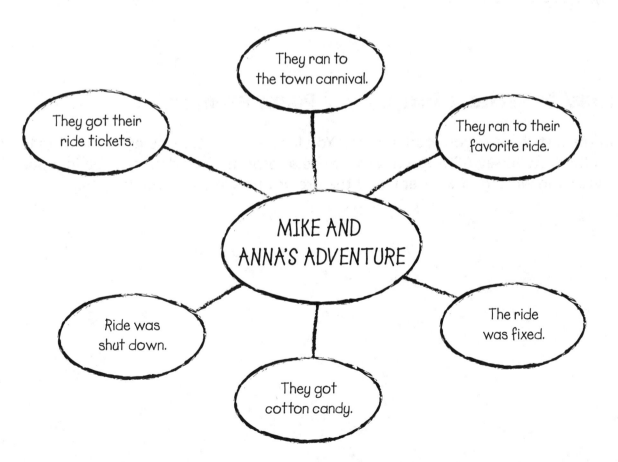

Now it's time to start writing. The following draft is a good draft. It's not perfect! But it's getting there.

After the school day ended Mike and Anna raced into town. They were so excited for their adventure to the carnival.

Soon, they finally arrived. They immediately ran over to the ticket booth to buy their ride tickets. After, they rushed over to their favorite ride, The Comet Coaster. When they got there they noticed a sign that said it was shut down.

Once they saw the sign they were very upset. So they asked the man working the ride how long it would be shut down for. He said one hour! Mike and Anna decided to get some cotton candy and walk around the carnival looking at all the sights. When they checked back at the Comet Coaster the ride was working!

Finally, the moment they were waiting for arrived. Mike and Anna enjoyed the rest of their day riding on the Comet Coaster.

What do you think? It's a good start, isn't it? Did you see any errors in the essay as you were reading it? There are a few. We'll fix these errors in a later section, "Revising."

How to Write a Draft for a Poem Prompt

In the last chapter, you read a poem. You learned that for one of the writing tasks on the New Jersey ASK, you have to write a response based on an idea in a poem. Here's the writing task, poem, and the prewriting we did in the last chapter.

Sample Writing Task

In "An Autumn Greeting," the poet writes about the leaves changing colors in the fall. In many states, the changing leaves signal the changing of the seasons from summer to fall. At one time or another, you have probably noticed some other signs that fall has arrived. Write a composition about other ways you can tell the seasons have changed from summer to fall.

In your composition, be sure to do the following:

- Describe at least two signs of fall.

- Explain how you can notice these signs.

- Tell how these signs make you feel about the changing of the seasons.

You may take notes, create a web, or do other prewriting work in the space provides on the blank pages. Then write your composition on the pages with lines.

An Autumn Greeting

Anonymous

"Come," said the Wind to the Leaves one day.
"Come over to the meadow and we will play.
Put on your dresses of red and gold.
For summer is gone and the days grow cold."

Signs of fall:

- The air starts to smell different.

- Kids go back to school.

- Stores have back-to-school sales.

- You start to want hot drinks like tea and apple cider.

- You start to wear jackets and sweaters at night.

- The air seems crisp and clear, not hazy and humid.

Creating a graphic organizer like the one below will help you when you are ready to write your essay.

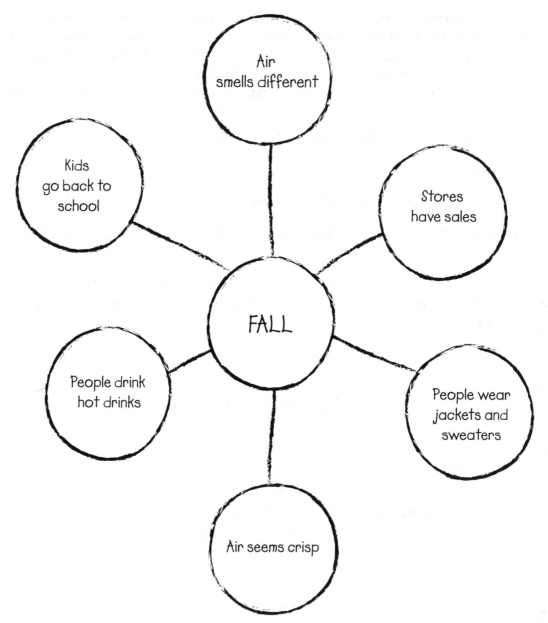

I love the fall! I can always tell when fall is coming the air smells really fresh. and it does not feel so hot anymore. We go back to school in the Fall. It is always fun to start a new school year. Before you know it, its time to wear jackets. People where sweaters, too. And, as the poem says, the leaves turn bright colors. It is so pretty! People drink hot drinks in the fall. Hot apple cider is my favorite.

What do you think of this essay? It is a good first draft. Do you see some errors? We'll fix these errors in the next section, "Revising."

Revising

When you revise your essay, you fix mistakes. You make sure that your essay is as good as it can be. Look at the writer's checklist below. The last two sentences are boldface. These sentences are about revising.

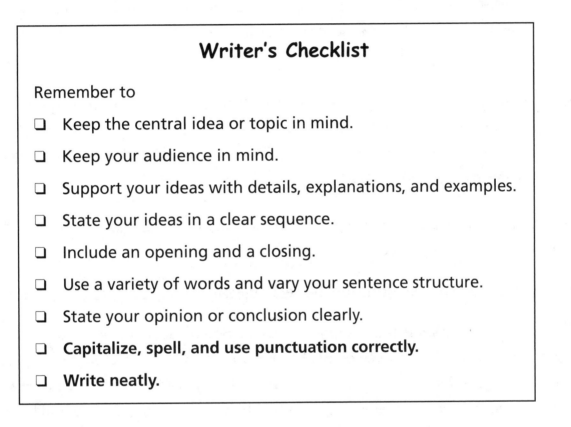

Writer's Checklist

Remember to

- ❑ Keep the central idea or topic in mind.
- ❑ Keep your audience in mind.
- ❑ Support your ideas with details, explanations, and examples.
- ❑ State your ideas in a clear sequence.
- ❑ Include an opening and a closing.
- ❑ Use a variety of words and vary your sentence structure.
- ❑ State your opinion or conclusion clearly.
- ❑ **Capitalize, spell, and use punctuation correctly.**
- ❑ **Write neatly.**

When you revise your essay, check to make sure that you have a capital letter at the beginning of each sentence. Street names should be capitalized. People's names should be, too. Seasons of the year are not capitalized, though. Also check to make sure that you have spelled all of your words correctly.

Make sure that each of your sentences has a period, an exclamation point, or a question mark after it. Make sure that you don't run two sentences into one and that each sentence in your essay is in fact complete and not just part of a sentence.

Notice the revisions in the first essay we wrote together.

After the school day ended , Mike and Anna raced into town. They were so excited about ~~for~~ their trip ~~adventure~~ to the carnival.

Soon, they finally arrived. They immediately ran over to the ticket booth to buy their ride tickets. Then ~~After,~~ they rushed over to their favorite ride, The Comet Coaster. When they got there they noticed a sign that said it was shut down.

When ~~Once~~ they saw the sign they were very upset. So they asked the man working the ride how long it would be shut down ~~for.~~ He said one hour! Mike and Anna decided to get some cotton candy and walk around the carnival to ~~looking~~ at all the sights. When they checked back at the Comet Coaster the ride was working!

Finally, the moment they were waiting for had arrived. Mike and Anna enjoyed the rest of their day riding on the Comet Coaster.

Now let's look at the revisions for the second essay.

I love the fall! I can always tell when fall is coming . T~~t~~he air smells really fresh , and it does not feel so hot anymore. We go back to school in the f~~F~~all. It is always fun to start a new school year. Before you know it, it 's time to wear jackets. People wear ~~where~~ sweaters, too. And, as the poem says, the leaves turn bright colors. It is so pretty! People drink hot drinks in the fall. Hot apple cider is my favorite.

New Jersey Assessment of Skills and Knowledge

LANGUAGE ARTS LITERACY — Grade 3

Practice Test 1

Writing Task 1

Using the prompt on page 120 as a guide, write a story about what might be happening.

You may take notes, create a web, or do other prewriting work in the space provided on pages 121 and 122. Then write your story on the lines provided on pages 123 and 124.

Here is a checklist for you to follow to help you do your best writing. Please read it silently as I read it aloud to you.

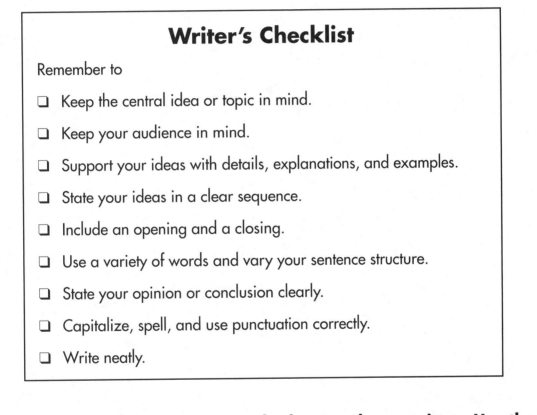

Writer's Checklist

Remember to

❑ Keep the central idea or topic in mind.

❑ Keep your audience in mind.

❑ Support your ideas with details, explanations, and examples.

❑ State your ideas in a clear sequence.

❑ Include an opening and a closing.

❑ Use a variety of words and vary your sentence structure.

❑ State your opinion or conclusion clearly.

❑ Capitalize, spell, and use punctuation correctly.

❑ Write neatly.

After you write your story, read what you have written. Use the checklist to make certain that your writing is the best it can be.

Two good friends were having an argument on the playground at lunch-time. They have decided that they would resolve their issue.

Directions: Write a story about the friends, their problem and what they do to fix it.

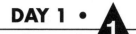

WRITING TASK 1 – PREWRITING SPACE
Use the space below and on page 122 to plan your writing.

- B playground Micker, Harry, Tommy.

- M ~~Mickey~~ They called the Tiny.

- E Macke Don ~~Mrs, Shell~~
Mrs. Robison.

WRITING TASK 1 – PREWRITING SPACE (continued)

Remember — your story must be written on the lines on pages 123 and 124 ONLY.

$\frac{8}{10}$

WRITING TASK 1

"Here comes play time!" exclaimed Mackie. It was recess time! Mackie and Don raced outside. They played on with the swings, and the monkey bars. Finally, it was time to play with the slides. The dilemma started.

Mackie and Don ran up the stairs and started sliding. Mackie sat first. Don wanted to be first so he pushed Mackie off the slide then he sat on the slide. Mackie pushed Don. This happened back and forth. The two brothers were watched by their parents father, Phillie Robinson. He saw their fight. Mackie and Don were in big trouble. When the brothers came back from school, they both were grounded for a week. They couldn't play video games, and fun activities for a week.

That's what Mackie and Don learned in the story. This also shows a story about two good friends who have a problem and what they do to fix it. Jackie and Don learned again, that never argue

WRITING TASK 1 (continued)

over petty things. n4

it is, but you should not argue.

If you have time, you may review your work in this section only.

STOP

**DO NOT GO ON
UNTIL YOU ARE
TOLD TO DO SO.**

Directions to the Student

Now you will read a story and answer the questions that follow. Some questions will be multiple choice; one will be open-ended.

1. You may look back at the reading passage as often as you want.

2. Read each question carefully and think about the answer.

3. For each multiple-choice question, select the best answer and fill in the circle next to your choice. Make sure you fill in the correct circle.

4. If you do not know the answer to a question, go on to the next question. You may come back to the skipped question later if you have time.

Directions: Read the story and answer the questions that follow.

A Trip of Tests

Long ago, New Jersey was a big forest. In that forest lived the Lenape people. The Lenape were kind people who worked hard. Some of them were farmers who grew food for everyone to eat. Other Lenape used trees and clay to make new houses for people to live in. Still others used animal skins to make warm clothes that would keep people comfortable in the cold winters.

On any day you might visit the Lenape, you'd find them all busy with their jobs. They were happy to work hard. Some sang songs and told jokes while they worked. But if you visited on one special day, you'd find the Lenape even happier than usual. That was the day they went to visit their neighbors on the other side of the forest.

Seke, who was nine, couldn't wait to make that special trip. He had been waiting all year to see his neighbors in the other village. Seke would be going there with his friends Wisawe and Mitsin, and all their parents.

Early one morning, the Lenape group started getting ready for their long trip. They knew they would have to walk a long way through the woods. They brought a lot of food to eat, and extra clothes in case it got cold. They wore their best moccasins to keep their feet safe from rocks and snakes. When they thought they had everything they would need, they started walking.

Seke and his friends were so excited they ran in circles around the group. They talked about their neighbors and all the fun things they would do when they reached them.

When night fell, the Lenape decided to make their camp in the forest. They rolled out their mats and then built a fire. They cooked some of their food and put the rest of it into a bag. They tied the bag to a high tree branch to keep it out of the reach of hungry bears.

After they ate, they all fell asleep quickly and dreamed of the fun they would soon have.

Late in the night, something growled in the woods. Wisawe's mother woke up and looked around. She could see a big black shape in the woods. It was a bear, sniffing the air and smelling the Lenape's food. The bear walked into the middle of the camp and stood tall on its legs. It was the tallest bear in the forest, and, reaching up, it could almost grab the food.

Wisawe's mother knew that they would need the food to make it through the forest. Thinking quickly, she jumped up and began clapping her hands. She began yelling, "Woo-woo! Hey, run away, bear!"

The bear was surprised by the woman and the loud sounds she was making. It growled again, but Wisawe's mother kept clapping and yelling. Scared, the bear stepped back, and then ran away from the camp. The food was safe.

Everyone was so proud of Wisawe's mother. She had been brave to protect the food from the hungry bear. Seke wished that *his* parents were that brave.

In the morning, the travelers had breakfast and then began walking again. The children's parents kept stopping to look around, talk, and point at different paths. Every path looked the same. It was soon clear that they were lost in the woods.

Just when it seemed that there was no way out, Mitsin's father called to the rest of them. "Look," he said, pointing at a break in the trees above them. "The sun is rising in the east."

Mitsin's father knew that the sun comes up on one side of the world and goes down on the other. By finding the sun, you can find out which way you're going. Since the Lenape knew they wanted to go east, they picked a path that went toward the sun.

Everyone thanked Mitsin's father for his help. He had been clever to learn how to find his way using the sun. Seke wished that *his* parents knew great things like that.

The Lenape stayed on that path, and soon they were no longer lost. They saw hills and trees that they had seen on their trip last year. Nobody was scared anymore, and everyone began joking and singing again.

Soon, though, they found that there was one last problem. There had been a lot of rain, and that rain had filled up a creek near the village. Now the creek was as full and wide as a river! The water ran cold and fast. Even the best swimmers in the Lenape group couldn't manage to swim all the way across the creek.

"We're stuck!" said Mitsin's father.

"There's no way to cross this creek," cried Wisawe's mother. "We'll have to go back home."

But this time, Seke's parents called out to the rest of them. "We can build a canoe to take us all to the other side," they said.

Nobody thought that they could do it. There were no tools around, or enough parts to make a good canoe. Even Seke wasn't sure that his parents could save them.

Seke's mother went to the side of the creek and gathered several round rocks. Seke's father banged the rocks together until they cracked. The cracked edges of the rocks were sharp, like axes.

Then Seke's parents went into the deep woods together and found a tall, tall tree. Seke's mother tied wet animal skins around the tree and then built a fire under them. The fire began to burn away at the tree trunk. The wet skins kept the rest of the tree from burning up. Soon the tree trunk was burnt and weak. Seke's father made an axe with a rock and chopped the tree down.

Seke's parents first pulled the bark off the tree. Then they cut a long hole into the middle of the tree. After many hours of hard work, they had made a canoe out of a tree!

All of the Lenape were able to sit inside the canoe, and they used tree branches to paddle their way across the creek. By the time night was falling, they were on the other side.

Their neighbors rushed from the village to meet them. Everyone smiled and hugged one another. They shared tales of their long trip through the forest. Everyone was proud of what Seke's parents had done—and Seke was sorry he had doubted them. He gave them both a big hug to thank them.

Then the Lenape had a wonderful time with their friends.

1. **At the beginning of the story, what happens on the Lenape's special day?**

   Ⓐ They use trees and clay to make new houses.

   Ⓑ They go across the forest to see their neighbors.

   Ⓒ They use animal skins to make warm clothes.

   Ⓓ They tell jokes and sing songs while they work.

2. **What is a theme of "A Trip of Tests"?**

   Ⓐ Being brave will always put you on top.

   Ⓑ Nature can teach us everything we need to know.

   Ⓒ Practicing something is the best way to succeed.

   Ⓓ Everyone has something important to offer.

3. **How does Mitsin's father help the group get to their neighbors' village?**

   Ⓐ He points out which path looks different than the others.

   Ⓑ He leads them in the right direction when they are lost.

   Ⓒ He gets them to move again after they keep stopping to talk.

   Ⓓ He gets the group to start laughing and singing again.

4.   How does Seke feel when Wisawe's mother scares away the bear?

Ⓐ He hopes that he will get a chance to scare a bear.

Ⓑ He wishes that he had been the first one to see the bear.

◉ He wishes his parents were as brave as she is.

Ⓓ He hopes that he will someday be so brave.

5.   Why do Seke's parents chop down a tree?

Ⓐ They want to build something for their neighbors.

Ⓑ They must stop a bear from stealing their food.

Ⓒ They want to show that they are useful, too.

◉ They must build a canoe to cross the big creek.

6.   In "A Trip of Tests," what does Seke learn about his parents?

◉ They are just as smart and brave as the other parents.

Ⓑ They do not know how to scare away a bear.

Ⓒ They do not know how to swim across a large creek.

Ⓓ They are greater than any other parents in the village.

For the open-ended question on the next page, remember to

- Focus your response on the question asked.
- Answer all parts of the question.
- Give a complete explanation.
- Use specific information from the story.

7. **During the trip to the neighbors' village, one or more of each child's parents must help the group continue on their journey.**

• **Explain how each parent helps the group.**

• **Decide which one is most helpful and why.**

Use information from the story to support your response. Write your answer on the lines below.

I think Wisawe's mother was really helpful because if she didn't save the food the Lenape's food, people would survie or may not live and the Lenapes might not gain energy. That's why I think Wisawe was really helpful.

If you have time, you may review your work in this section only.

STOP

DO NOT GO ON UNTIL YOU ARE TOLD TO DO SO.

Directions to the Student

Now you will read a story and answer the questions that follow. Some questions will be multiple choice; one will be open-ended.

1. You may look back at the reading passage as often as you want.

2. Read each question carefully and think about the answer.

3. For each multiple-choice question, select the best answer and fill in the circle next to your choice. Make sure you fill in the correct circle.

4. If you do not know the answer to a question, go on to the next question. You may come back to the skipped question later if you have time.

Directions: Read the passage below. Then answer the questions about the passage.

Down the Drain

Jason stopped in the middle of his walk home from school. He listened carefully, then asked himself, "What is that noise? It sounds like cheeping."

Studying the trees, Jason didn't see any nests. Then he heard the cheeping again.

"What's going on?" asked Kimmy.

"Listen! Can you hear that?" Jason asked.

Kimmy strained to hear anything unusual. Then she said, "It sounds like baby birds to me. They sure sound funny though."

"Yeah," said Jason. "They sound like they're inside something."

Jason and Kimmy started looking around. Keeshon stopped his bike at the curb. "Did you guys lose something?"

"No, we're looking for baby birds," Jason said.

Keeshon got off his bike and started hunting too. "The cheeping seems to be coming from over here," he said.

Jason and Kimmy stooped down and heard the noise too. "Oh my gosh!" Jason said. "They're in the storm drain! There's no way we can get them out. What are we going to do?"

"First, we're going to run," said Kimmy. "Here comes an angry mother duck!"

The three friends dashed onto Mrs. Uchida's front porch. The angry duck stopped short of the porch and wouldn't let them come down.

"What's all the noise?" asked Mrs. Uchida, opening her door and stepping outside.

Quickly Jason told the story. "Have you got any ideas, Mrs. Uchida?"

"Well, fire fighters rescue cats from trees all the time. Maybe they can rescue ducklings from a storm drain. Wait here, and I'll phone them."

The fire truck came down the street and stopped by the curb. The roar of the engine helped the people on the porch. It seemed to scare the mother duck. She flew up to the roof and sat on the peak. Mrs. Uchida and the children rushed to the fire truck.

"Where's the storm drain with the ducklings?" asked the fire chief.

"Right over here," said Jason, walking to the spot. "The ducklings somehow got into the drain. We can't see them, but they sure are noisy."

All the fire fighters gathered together and checked out the storm drain. At last the chief said, "Get a ladder and a tool to remove the grate from the top of the drain."

A couple of fire fighters quickly obeyed the chief. Soon they had the grate off the drain. Then they placed the ladder into the opening.

The chief said, "Hanson, you're pretty skinny. Climb down there and see what you can do."

Hanson pulled off his coat and laid aside his helmet. He slowly went down the ladder. At the bottom he turned left and looked inside the pipe that carried rainwater away. "Here they are," he called.

A few moments later, Hanson climbed back up the ladder. He carried a bag that had been slung over his shoulder before.

Everyone crowded around. They could see nine baby ducks inside the bag. They were still cheeping away. Loud quacking made everyone glance up. The mother duck was flapping her wings and having a fit up on the roof.

The fire chief took the bag to the park across the street. He carefully lifted out each duckling and placed it on the ground near the pond. When he was finished, he walked back to the fire truck. The mother duck swooped down from the roof and landed beside her children. They crowded around her. Then she led them to the pond and they swam away.

"Wow!" said Jason. "Sometimes fire fighters get to save lives and have fun at the same time. That sounds like a great job!"

"It is," smiled the chief.

8. **What is the first thing Jason does in this story?**

    Ⓐ stops on his way home from school

    Ⓑ talks with his friends

    Ⓒ looks in the drain

    Ⓓ runs from the mother duck

9. **What causes Jason to check out the storm drain?**

    Ⓐ He hears a cheeping noise coming from the drain.

    Ⓑ He drops his book in the storm drain.

    Ⓒ He sees the mother duck on the drain.

    Ⓓ He hears water running in the drain.

10. **How are the baby ducks different from their mother?**

    Ⓐ They chase people.

    Ⓑ They are not very old.

    ● They can't swim.

    Ⓓ They are not very loud.

11. Which of the following is a fact from the story?

Ⓐ No one is afraid of ducks.

Ⓑ Fire fighters save cats too.

Ⓒ Jason's parents are angry that he is late.

Ⓓ Kimmy is Jason's best friend.

12. Which opinion, or feeling, do all the characters share?

Ⓐ They dislike loud noises like sirens.

Ⓑ They hate angry ducks.

Ⓒ They want to be fire fighters.

● They care about the baby ducks.

13. Why did the fire fighters quickly obey the chief?

Ⓐ They were afraid of him.

Ⓑ They didn't know what to do.

● Fire fighters all have to listen to one leader so that everyone stays safe.

Ⓓ He was the only one who knew what to do.

For the open-ended question on the next page, remember to

- **Focus your response on the question asked.**

- **Answer all parts of the question.**

- **Give a complete explanation.**

- **Use specific information from the story.**

14. Why did the mother duck chase the children up onto the porch? Why did Hanson carry the baby ducks to the park across the street?

Use information from the story to support your response. Write your answer on the lines below.

The mother duck chased the children up onto the porch because she thought they would hurt them and protect them. Hanson carried the baby ducks to the park across the street because her mother was waiting for him and she also cares for her baby ducklings. Only somebody who is a gentleman or women who cares about nature.

If you have time, you may review your work in this section only.

STOP

CLOSE YOUR BOOK.

Directions to the Student

Read the poem "The Land of Counterpane" to yourself while I read it aloud to you. Afterward, you will do a writing task. The poem may give you ideas for your writing.

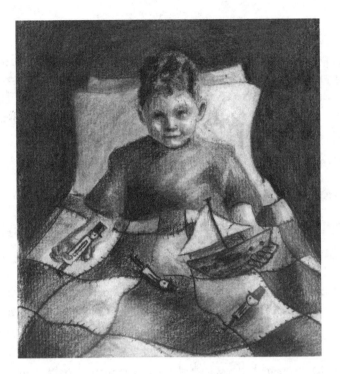

The Land of Counterpane

by Robert Louis Stevenson

When I was sick and lay a-bed,
I had two pillows at my head,
And all my toys beside me lay
To keep me happy all the day.

And sometimes for an hour or so
I watched my leaden soldiers go,
With different uniforms and drills,
Among the bedclothes, through the hills;

And sometimes sent my ships in fleets
All up and down among the sheets;
Or brought my trees and houses out,
And planted cities all about.

I was the giant great and still
That sits upon the pillow-hill,
And sees before him, dale and plain,
The pleasant land of counterpane.[1]

[1]**counterpane:** a quilt, blanket, or bedspread.

Writing Task 2

In "The Land of Counterpane," the poet Robert Louis Stevenson writes about a child playing with toys while he is sick. At one time or another, most of us have been sick in bed or have needed something fun to do and used our imaginations to amuse ourselves. Write a composition about how you have used your imagination to amuse yourself.

In your composition, be sure to do the following:

- **Describe what it is that you imagine.**

- **Explain what you use to make your imaginary play seem more real.**

- **Discuss how it is valuable for a child to have a good imagination.**

You may take notes, create a web, or do other prewriting work in the space provided on pages 147 and 148. Then write your composition on the lines provided on pages 149 and 150.

Here is a checklist for you to follow to help you do your best writing. Please read it silently as I read it aloud to you.

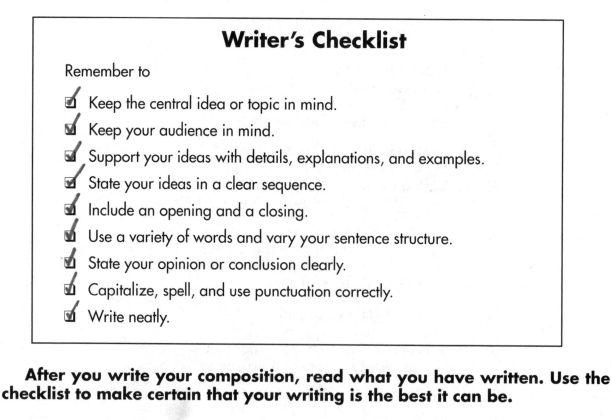

Writer's Checklist

Remember to

☑ Keep the central idea or topic in mind.

☑ Keep your audience in mind.

☑ Support your ideas with details, explanations, and examples.

☑ State your ideas in a clear sequence.

☑ Include an opening and a closing.

☑ Use a variety of words and vary your sentence structure.

☑ State your opinion or conclusion clearly.

☑ Capitalize, spell, and use punctuation correctly.

☑ Write neatly.

After you write your composition, read what you have written. Use the checklist to make certain that your writing is the best it can be.

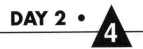
WRITING TASK 2 – PREWRITING SPACE
Use the space below and on page 148 to plan your writing.

WRITING TASK 2 – PREWRITING SPACE (continued)

B ME✓ ~~Bed~~✓

M Got sick, ✓

E Had medicne ✓

I can't talk.

Remember — your composition must be written on the lines on
pages 149 and 150 ONLY.

WRITING TASK 2

All day long I had the blues, nothing else
to do. The light swicted so bright. Sh. M
Mom came, but acted said. She said "Being
lame is not how you react. You should listen
and respect everbody." I thought about
last time when dad gave my itchy medicine.
He helped me when I was ill. "Imagining
can you help you when your are ill because
you can imagine an eexperince you had
and can solve your promblem!" I said.
Finally, I had medicine and got better You
used your mind said Mom. That's how you
solved a problem!"

WRITING TASK 2 (continued)

_____

_____

_____

_____

_____

_____

_____

_____

_____

_____

_____

_____

_____

_____

_____

_____

_____

If you have time, you may review your work in this section only.

STOP

**DO NOT GO ON
UNTIL YOU ARE
TOLD TO DO SO.**

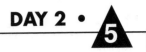

Directions to the Student

In the following section, you will read a passage and answer the questions that follow.

Some questions will be multiple choice; one will be open-ended.

1. You may look back at the reading passage as often as you want.

2. Read each question carefully and think about the answer.

3. For each multiple-choice question, select the best answer and fill in the circle next to your choice. Make sure you fill in the correct circle.

4. If you do not know the answer to a question, go on to the next question. You may come back to the skipped question later if you have time.

Directions: Read the article and answer the questions that follow.

Chickasaw Day Camp

Joining the happy campers at Chickasaw Day Camp is the perfect way to make the most of your summer! While some children go to special camps for different interests, Camp Chickasaw offers a little bit of everything, so campers don't have to choose—they can do it all!

Camp counselors at Chickasaw Day Camp are not only your leaders; they are also your friends. Each group leader and activity leader is responsible for a group of fifteen campers. Your counselor will be your leader for the whole summer.

Campers are picked up on buses that arrive at the camp at eight o'clock each morning. From the buses, campers report to their cabins to prepare for the day's activities. Group leaders make sure that each child has the right clothing and other things needed for that day.

NOTE: Parents will receive a list of all clothing and other things that their child will need for each day of camp. Your child's group leader will call you if the list changes at all throughout the summer.

Group counselors take the group the first activity of the day. When the activity is over, group leaders gather their group and take them to their next event. Look at all there is to do at Chickasaw Day Camp:

 Whether you know how to play music or want to learn, Camp Chickasaw can help. We offer a wonderful music program for both beginning and advanced musicians. Our music teacher and group leaders are experienced at playing many different kinds of musical instruments. We have some instruments here at the camp. Others should be brought by campers. Call ahead before signing up campers for music.

 Want to express yourself through art? Many young artists have got-ten their start right here at Chickasaw Day Camp. Campers will learn how to paint with watercolors, oils, and poster paints. They will also take drawing lessons.

Do you love to get moving to a beat? Our dance teachers are skilled in all different kinds of dance. A new kind of dance class is offered every two weeks.

If you play it, we've got it. Chickasaw Day Camp offers many different kinds of sports.

Know how to swim already? Want to learn? Camp Chickasaw offers swimming lessons for different levels and age groups all day long. We have four pools at our camp. This allows us to offer swimming lessons and free swims at all times throughout the day. All group leaders and activity leaders have been trained to make sure that campers are safe whenever they are in the pool.

Nothing beats riding a horse on a beautiful summer day! Younger children can ride ponies in a field on campgrounds, while older children can ride adult horses on wooded trails. Campers will also learn how to care for horses. This activity is a camper favorite.

How good are your computer skills? Could they be better? Our classes can help you improve. Campers can learn how to design video games and Web pages. They can post messages for other campers, or send e-mails to family and friends. We also teach our campers about Internet safety.

Do you know your way around the woods? We take campers on daily nature walks so they can get exercise while learning about nature. We teach campers about the birds, plants, and animals that live in the forest around the camp.

Being on the water is a great feeling. Children and their activity leaders can take long boat rides around Lake Jeanine, which lies right on the edge of the camp. Leaders will take small groups of children out onto the lake in rowboats and sailboats.

Ever catch a fish? Did you eat it? We have some of the best fishing in the state here at Camp Chickasaw. Campers will learn all about fishing in these classes. Leaders will then cook the fish that campers have caught. The camp hosts a fish fry once a week.

As you can see, Camp Chickasaw has so much to do that its campers are sure to be happy!

Campers will be served lunch every day. Campers also eat a little something in the afternoon to hold them over until dinnertime. Children will receive a camp menu when they sign up for camp. Parents, please tell leaders if your child cannot eat a certain food for one reason or another. We will arrange to have another meal prepared for your child.

If you are interested in joining the Camp Chickasaw family, please sign up today! We will send you a booklet with all of the information you need to get your summer started right!

Chickasaw

Day Camp

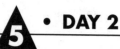

15. What does the word "improve" mean in the following sentence: "Our classes can help you improve"?

Ⓐ know

Ⓑ fall into

Ⓒ tell

Ⓓ get better

16. Which lessons are offered throughout the whole day?

Ⓐ boating

Ⓑ horseback riding

Ⓒ swimming

Ⓓ painting

17. The purpose of the first paragraph is to

Ⓐ introduce the idea that Camp Chickasaw is great for children.

Ⓑ give children a list of things they can do at Camp Chickasaw.

Ⓒ explain why some children go to special camps for different interests.

Ⓓ explain how parents can find out more about different day camps.

18. What is the purpose of calling ahead before signing up for music classes?

Ⓐ to see whether campers can bring their music teachers from home ✗

Ⓑ to ask whether the camp offers any kind of music classes ✗

Ⓒ to find out whether campers need to bring an instrument to camp ✗

Ⓓ to tell the camp how you think music lessons should be taught

19. What does the word "responsible" mean in the third paragraph of the passage?

Ⓐ in charge ✗

Ⓑ look at ✗

Ⓒ order around ✗

Ⓓ act like ✗

20. Which would be best if you were tired?

Ⓐ sports ✗

Ⓑ computers

Ⓒ dance ✗

Ⓓ swimming ✗

For the open-ended question on the next page, remember to

- Focus your response on the question asked.
- Answer all parts of the question.
- Give a complete explanation.
- Use specific information from the story.

21. Explain the reasons that children will need different kinds of clothing for different days at camp. Use information from the article to support your response. Write your answer on the lines below.

Children will need different types of
clothing like shorts for summer in camp.
You can wear even t-shirts and shirts
From "Diary of a _____ it said that
sweat pant would be good for summer
In winter, I would wear warm cozzy
clothing _____ There are many
_____ For fall it _____ to get
cold _____ like in winter _____
a _____ and to _____ the
full name of the diary is "Diary
_____ It says _____
that _____ pants to gym. In sport
it _____ You may feel
hot _____ For cold weather sporty
clothing you can wear in camp is _____
clothing _____ in camp.

If you have time, you may review your work in this section only. STOP

CLOSE YOUR BOOK.

New Jersey Assessment of Skills and Knowledge

LANGUAGE ARTS LITERACY   Grade 3

Practice Test 2

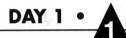

Writing Task 1

Using the prompt on page 162 as a guide, write a story about what might be happening.

You may take notes, create a web, or do other prewriting work in the space provided on pages 163 and 164. Then write your story on the lines provided on pages 165 and 166.

Here is a checklist for you to follow to help you do your best writing. Please read it silently as I read it aloud to you.

Writer's Checklist

Remember to

❑ Keep the central idea or topic in mind.

❑ Keep your audience in mind.

❑ Support your ideas with details, explanations, and examples.

❑ State your ideas in a clear sequence.

❑ Include an opening and a closing.

❑ Use a variety of words and vary your sentence structure.

❑ State your opinion or conclusion clearly.

❑ Capitalize, spell, and use punctuation correctly.

❑ Write neatly.

After you write your story, read what you have written. Use the checklist to make certain that your writing is the best it can be.

TURN TO THE NEXT PAGE. ➡

The last day of school was near. All of the students were excited for summer vacation. Joe had been planning his first day off from school. He could not wait. Then without warning something changed all of his careful planning.

Write a story about what happened to change his plans.

You may take notes, create a web, or do other prewriting work in the space provided. Then, write your description on the lines provided.

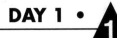
WRITING TASK 1 — PREWRITING SPACE
Use the space below and on page 162 to plan your writing.

B   Yeah

M

E

WRITING TASK 1 – PREWRITING SPACE (continued)

Remember — your story must be written on the lines on pages
165 and 166 ONLY.

WRITING TASK 1

"Yeah! No school tommorow!" Joe was so
excited. He decided that he should go to Disney
land. He told it to Johnnyoobery, his best friends.
He asked it if it was okay. Joe replied sure. When
Joe came he saw his Mom wasn't in the living
room. Next, he checked the kitchen. She wasn't
there, either. Then, he checked the guest room.
No sign of her in there. After. that, he checked
the computer room. He only heard a ill noise. It
came from the sleeping room. Mom was sleeping
had an ice pack on her head. These clues show
that Joe's mom is sick. Joe can't go to D...
Disneyland without his mother. He loves his
mother and can't let her stay home and on the
other hand... she is sick! Therefore, Joe has
to change his plans about going to Osneyland
and stay back with is mother.

These reasons why Joe would stay back.
They also support why. These reasons even show

WRITING TASK 1 (continued)

the personality of Joe.

_____

_____

_____

_____

_____

_____

_____

_____

_____

_____

_____

_____

_____

_____

_____

If you have time, you may review your work in this section only.

STOP

**DO NOT GO ON
UNTIL YOU ARE
TOLD TO DO SO.**

Directions to the Student

Now you will read a story and answer the questions that follow.

Some questions will be multiple choice; one will be open-ended.

1. You may look back at the reading passage as often as you want.

2. Read each question carefully and think about the answer.

3. For each multiple-choice question, select the best answer and fill in the circle next to your choice. Make sure you fill in the correct circle.

4. If you do not know the answer to a question, go on to the next question. You may come back to the skipped question later if you have time.

Directions: Read the story and answer the questions that follow.

Important Promises

"Galen, you promised you would clean your room today."

"I'll do it later, Dad. I promise."

Galen skipped out the door and got her bike out of the garage. It was a beautiful sunny day, not the kind of day that a kid wanted to spend cleaning her room. Galen wanted to be outside, to have fun with her friends. So she rode her bike down the street to her neighbor Patty's house.

"Hey, Galen! Come on in the pool!" Patty yelled, so Galen parked her bike in the yard and eagerly jumped into the cold water. Cleaning her room was the furthest thing from her mind.

Later Galen and Patty ate hot dogs and drank lemonade. Then they decided to call their friend Mike to see if he wanted to play baseball in the park.

"Sure, I'll meet you there," Mike told them. So Galen walked home to get her baseball bat. Her mother was watering the grass.

"Oh, good, you're home," she said. "Now you can clean your room."

"Oh, I will, Mom. I promise. But first I want to play baseball with my friends."

Galen's mother frowned. "You do know that a promise is an important thing," she said. "If you promise to do something, you should do it."

"I promise I will," Galen told her. "But first I want to have fun with my friends."

Galen went to her room and got her baseball, her baseball bat, and her glove. Then she went to meet her friends at the park.

They played baseball until the sun went down. Galen rode her bike home fast. If she wasn't home for dinner, her parents would be worried.

When she walked into the house, her parents were putting dinner on the table. They didn't look happy, but they didn't say anything to her about her unclean room.

After dinner, Galen went up to her room. She looked around at the clothes and toys and books on the floor and all over the place. She thought about cleaning up, but she had a full belly and was tired. So instead, she pushed the mess on her bed onto the floor, lay down on her bed, and fell asleep.

The next morning, Patty called.

"Hi, Galen," Patty said, sounding sad. "I can't find my cat, Mr. Stripes. Can you help me look for him?"

Galen felt bad for Patty, so she said, "Sure, Patty. I promise I'll be over soon."

Galen stepped over everything on her floor and made her way to the bathroom. She washed up, went downstairs, and took a bowl of cereal outside to eat in the sunshine. It was a hot day, and Galen knew that she would much rather sit in her cold house than walk around the neighborhood in the hot sun. She also knew that she had promised Patty she would help her look for her cat and that she should do it, but she didn't want to.

"She's probably already found him by now," Galen thought. "I'll just stay home and finish that book I've been reading." As she read, her eyes started to get heavy, and before she knew it, she was asleep.

Galen woke up to her little sister, Beatrice, tugging on her arm.

"Galen, I need help with my math homework," she said.

Galen yawned. "Okay, Bea, but not right now. I promise I'll help you later, okay?"

Beatrice frowned. "You always promise you're going to do things, and then you never do them."

Galen laughed. "That's not true, Bea. I promise I'll help you in a little bit. Don't worry."

Beatrice walked away pouting, and Galen went back to her nap.

When she woke up, her parents, Patty, and Beatrice were all standing in front of her chair. Her parents looked mad, and Patty and Beatrice looked sad. Galen shook her head to make sure she wasn't dreaming.

"Galen, did you promise Patty that you would help her find her cat?" he asked.

Galen looked at Patty and nodded, but she looked away.

"And did you do it?"

Galen shook her head.

"Did you promise your sister that you would help her with her math homework?" her mother asked. Galen looked at Beatrice and nodded, but she looked away, too.

"And did you do it?"

Galen shook her head.

"You also promised us you would clean your room yesterday, and I'd be willing to bet that it still isn't clean. Did you clean your room?" Galen's father asked.

Now Galen looked at the ground.

"You have made promises to all of us, and you have let us all down by not following through on those promises," Galen's mother said. "You should never make a promise that you don't plan on keeping. A promise is a special thing. It is a way to tell someone that they can depend on you, that you will be there to help them if they need you. If you make promises and don't keep them, it says that you cannot be depended on, that you are not willing to help your friends and family when they need you."

"A broken promise is far worse than not promising anything in the first place," said Galen's father. Galen knew he was right. She was ashamed that she let down her family and her friend.

"I'm sorry. I'll fix it. I promise," she said. No one looked happy to hear it. "Really, I promise. Patty, let's go look for Mr. Stripes. Then, after we find him, Beatrice, I'll help you with your homework. When your homework is done, I'll clean my room. I promise!"

Galen jumped up, grabbed Patty's hand, and pulled her out the door. Patty was still mad, but she wanted to find her cat. The two of them walked around the neighborhood, calling Mr. Stripes's name. Finally, they heard a loud meow from behind a neighbor's bush.

"Mr. Stripes!" Patty scooped up her cat and hugged him tightly. Then she thanked Galen for finally following through on her promise.

"You're welcome. I'm glad I could help you, but now I have to go help my sister."

When Galen got home, Beatrice was sitting at the kitchen table with her math book in front of her. She hadn't written anything on her paper. Galen sat down next to her and explained her math problems to her. When they finished, Beatrice smiled and thanked her.

Then Galen ran upstairs and started cleaning her room. By the time she was done, she was so tired she went to bed. Then her parents knocked on her door. The looks on their faces told Galen that they were happy.

"How do you feel now that you've followed through on all of the promises you made?" Galen's father asked.

Galen smiled sleepily. "Really tired! But I feel good. I never meant to break promises, and now I understand the importance of a promise," she said.

Her parents said good night and turned out the light, and Galen drifted off into a deep sleep.

 TURN TO THE NEXT PAGE.

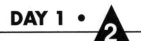

1. **At the beginning of the story, why doesn't Galen clean her room?**

   Ⓐ She wants to take a nap.

   Ⓑ She wants to read a book.

   Ⓒ She wants to play outside.

   Ⓓ She wants to help her sister.

2. **What does the word "ashamed" mean in the following sentence: "She was ashamed that she let down her family and her friend"?**

   Ⓐ proud

   Ⓑ angry

   Ⓒ sorry

   Ⓓ scared

3. **What lesson does Galen learn in "Important Promises"?**

   Ⓐ It's important to help your family and your friends.

   Ⓑ It's important to keep your room clean.

   Ⓒ It's important to do what you say you are going to do.

   Ⓓ It's important to spend time playing outside.

4. **Where does the end of this story take place?**

   Ⓐ in Galen's bedroom

   Ⓑ at the kitchen table

   Ⓒ in Patty's pool

   Ⓓ in Galen's living room

5. **What is a theme of "Important Promises"?**

   Ⓐ You should help others.

   Ⓑ You should not make promises.

   Ⓒ You should keep promises.

   Ⓓ You should listen to your parents.

6. **The purpose of the last paragraph is to**

   Ⓐ teach a lesson about helping people.

   Ⓑ show that Galen has learned a lesson.

   Ⓒ explain how Galen feels after working.

   Ⓓ describe what is it like to learn a lesson.

For the open-ended question on the next page, remember to

- **Focus your response on the question asked.**
- **Answer all parts of the question.**
- **Give a complete explanation.**
- **Use specific information from the story.**

7. **In the story, Galen makes an important promise to her parents, to Patty, and to Beatrice.**

   • **Explain each promise that Galen makes.**

   • **Decide which one is the most important and why.**

   Use information from the story to support your answer. Write your answer on the lines below.

3/4

The first promise that Galen made is to her parents is that she had to clean her room. In the story the author states "Galen, you promised you would clean your room today. I'll do it later Dad. I promise." This shows a promise that Galen makes. Galen also made her promise to her friend Patty that she would help find her cat named Mr. Stripes. Lastly, she made a promise to his her little sister, Beatrice.

The one that is the most important is Galen's promise to Beatrice. That is the most important one because if Galen didn't tell Beatrice the answers, she couldn't finish her homework. In

→ continue

If you have time, you may review your work in this section only.

STOP

Directions to the Student

Read the expository prompt on the next page.

the story it states "Galen woke up to her little sister, Beatrice, tugging on her arm. "Galen, I need help with my math homework," she said. Beatrice frowned. "You always promise you're going to do things, and then ya never do them." When she woke up, her parents, Patty, and Beatrice were all standing in front of her chair." This shows that this one is the most important, and it supports why. This reminds me of a piece of text called "A Messy Kid" because in both stories, both children were really lazy.

Many people would like to have a chance to go up into space. Pretend that you were able to take a trip into space last summer. Tell about your trip into space.

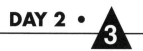
Writing Task 2

In your composition, be sure to do the following:

- **Describe how the trip started.**

- **Tell of some of the adventures you had.**

- **Tell what it was like when you got back to Earth.**

You may take notes, create a web, or do other prewriting work in the space provided on pages 182 and 183. Then write your composition on the lines provided on pages 184 and 185.

Here is a checklist for you to follow to help you do your best writing. Please read it silently as I read it aloud to you.

Writer's Checklist

Remember to

❑ Keep the central idea or topic in mind.

❑ Keep your audience in mind.

❑ Support your ideas with details, explanations, and examples.

❑ State your ideas in a clear sequence.

❑ Include an opening and a closing.

❑ Use a variety of words and vary your sentence structure.

❑ State your opinion or conclusion clearly.

❑ Capitalize, spell, and use punctuation correctly.

❑ Write neatly.

After you write your composition, read what you have written. Use the checklist to make certain that your writing is the best it can be.

WRITING TASK 2— PREWRITING SPACE

Use the space below and on page 183 to plan your writing.

B-Enter ~~Ship~~ shuttle

M-

E-

WRITING TASK 2— PREWRITING SPACE (continued)

Remember—your composition must be written on the lines on
pages 184 and 185 *only*.

8.1/10

WRITING TASK 2

Last Sunday, we went in the space shuttle!
We had to practice first. There is no gravity in
space. Therefore, we had a lot of training to float
in the air. We had to wear a special space
suit. We were excited when the space shuttle
took of from the Earth station. The lift off
was so smooth. from the launch pad that we
did not feel any jerks or bumps. During our
During our flight to space, the captian told
us about the space station and gave us
instructions what to do in the space station. In
the space station, it was a wonderful insperiance
to see the activites of the astronauts and how
they spent their time. When we looked from the
space station through the Earth, we realized Earth
is the most beautiful planet in the solar
system.
After a few days, we started are preperation
for are journey to the Earth. We put on our

WRITING TASK 2 (continued)

Space suit and got ready for the travel to Earth. Our landing to Earth was very smooth. The space shuttle landed like an airplane. We came out of the space shuttle and everybody cheered us. Before we were allowed to go home, we were throughly examined medically. It was once in a life time experince for me.

If you have time, you may review your work in this section only.

STOP

DO NOT GO ON
UNTIL YOU ARE
TOLD TO DO SO.

Directions to the Student

In the following section, you will read a passage and answer the questions that follow.

Some questions will be multiple choice; one will be open-ended.

1. You may look back at the reading passage as often as you want.

2. Read each question carefully and think about the answer.

3. For each multiple-choice question, select the best answer and fill in the circle next to your choice. Make sure you fill in the correct circle.

4. If you do not know the answer to a question, go on to the next question. You may come back to the skipped question later if you have time.

How to Grow Sunflowers

Have you ever seen a sunflower? Sunflowers are huge! Some sunflowers grow up to seven feet tall. This is much taller than a person.

Sunflowers are very beautiful. And the seeds in the flower can be roasted, salted, and eaten. If you don't want to eat the seeds, you can feed them to the birds. Sunflowers are easy to grow if you follow these steps.

Step 1: Find a Good Place

Find a good place to plant sunflower seeds. Sunflowers need lots of sun, so look for a spot that gets lots of bright sunshine. When sunflowers get tall, their stems break easily if the wind blows. So, if you can, look for a sunny spot near a fence or a wall. A fence or wall will help protect sunflowers from the wind. If you have a large yard, try planting seeds in a few different areas. This will help you tell where sunflowers grow best. If you have a small yard, try planting sunflowers in patio boxes or large pots.

Step 2: Gather Your Supplies

To grow sunflowers, you need to buy sunflower seeds! There are many different kinds of sunflowers and seeds. Giant sunflowers grow the tallest. You'll also need a small shovel to plant your seeds. A ruler is helpful, too. A bag of peat will help make the soil good for growing. Peat is a type of dirt. You can buy peat at a garden or discount store.

You Will Need—

Sunflower seeds

A small shovel or large spoon

A ruler

A small bag of peat

A few tall sticks

Flower fertilizer

Scissors

String

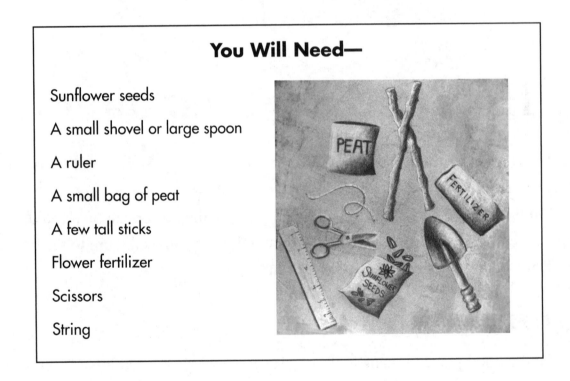

Step 3: Wait for the Right Time

It's important to plant sunflowers when the weather is warm enough for them to grow. It's best to wait until after the last frost. May is a good month to plant sunflowers in most places.

Step 4: Plant Carefully

Before you plant, you need to get the soil ready. Mix up the soil a little with your shovel, and mix in some of the peat. If the soil is very dry, add a little bit of water. Push the seeds about one inch into the ground. Plant the seeds six inches apart. (You can use your ruler to do this.) Water the seeds well after you plant them. If you have a lot of birds in your yard, cover your seeds with an old screen. This will keep birds and small animals from digging the seeds out of the ground.

Step 5: Thin the Plants

Sunflowers grow very quickly. You should see small plants in about a week. You'll notice that some plants are smaller than others. The larger plants will grow into the biggest, healthiest sunflowers. Thin out the smaller plants. When you thin your flowers, you pull them out. This makes more room for the roots of the healthier plants to grow. Thin your sunflowers so that they are about 1½ feet apart. Sunflower plants grow slow at first, but they pick up speed in time.

Step 6: Water, Feed, and Stake the Plants

Keep the soil wet, but not soaked. Water your sunflower plants a little bit each day when it doesn't rain. You might also want to feed your plants fertilizer from time to time.

Sometimes the flower on the sunflower gets heavier than the stem. When this happens, the sunflower might tip over or lean to one side. Your sunflowers might also lean toward the sun. Staking your sunflowers will help keep them standing straight. When you stake a sunflower, you simply tie it to a stick or to the fence. Don't put the stick too close to the sunflower. You don't want to damage the sunflower's roots. Tie the sunflower loosely to the stick with a piece of string. Tying the string too tight might damage the sunflower's stem.

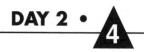
Step 7: Harvest the Seeds

In the fall the flower in the center of your sunflower will shrivel and turn brown. This is the time to harvest the sunflower's seeds. Ask a grown-up to cut the flower part of the sunflower off. Then put it someplace dry where it can dry out. When it is dry, take out the seeds in the center of the flower. A grown-up can help you sprinkle the seeds with salt and roast them. Or you can put them in your yard for the birds to enjoy. You can also keep the dry seeds to plant in the spring of the next year.

8. **The purpose of the first paragraph is to**

Ⓐ give a summary of how to plant sunflowers.

Ⓑ introduce the reader to the sunflower.

Ⓒ convince the reader to plant sunflower seeds.

Ⓓ describe a good place to plant sunflowers.

9. **What item is used to keep a sunflower from bending and breaking?**

Ⓐ ruler

Ⓑ stick

Ⓒ shovel

Ⓓ spoon

10. **What is the purpose of the peat?**

Ⓐ to give the sunflower plants food

Ⓑ to keep the sunflower seeds safe

Ⓒ to make sunflowers stand up straight

Ⓓ to make dirt good for growing

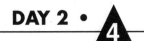

11. What does "soaked" mean in the following sentence: "Keep the soil wet, but not soaked"?

Ⓐ dried out

Ⓑ clean

Ⓒ very wet

Ⓓ a little wet

12. What does the word "harvest" mean in the last paragraph of the article?

Ⓐ gather

Ⓑ plant

Ⓒ move

Ⓓ cook

13. The author probably wrote this article to

Ⓐ teach readers how to plant sunflower seeds.

Ⓑ describe what it is like to grow sunflowers.

Ⓒ teach readers how to eat sunflower seeds.

Ⓓ entertain readers with a story about sunflowers.

For the open-ended question on the next page, remember to

- **Focus your response on the question asked.**

- **Answer all parts of the question.**

- **Give a complete explanation.**

- **Use specific information from the story.**

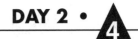
14. Explain the reasons you should thin out sunflower plants. Use information from the article to support your response. Write your answer on the lines below.

You should thin out sunflower plants because it makes room for the healthier plants to grow. In the story it says "Thin out the smaller plants. When you thin your flowers, you pull them out. This makes more room for the roots of the healthier plants to grow. Thin your sunflowers so that they are about 1½ feet apart. Sunflower plants grow slow at first but they pick up speed in time." This shows why you should thin out sunflower plants and these also show something else too. This also tells why you should do so. This reminds me of a story called "Sunflowers and How to Plant Sunflowers." I say so because it talks about how to grow sunflowers and the steps to make it grow just like this story does. Here steps to make sunflowers.

If you have time, you may review your work in this section only.

DO NOT GO ON
UNTIL YOU ARE
TOLD TO DO SO.

Directions to the Student

In the following section, you will read a passage and answer the questions that follow.

Some questions will be multiple choice; one will be open-ended.

1. You may look back at the reading passage as often as you want.

2. Read each question carefully and think about the answer.

3. For each multiple-choice question, select the best answer and fill in the circle next to your choice. Make sure you fill in the correct circle.

4. If you do not know the answer to a question, go on to the next question. You may come back to the skipped question later if you have time.

Make a
Papier-Mâché Mask

1 Gather the following ingredients: ½ cup of flour, 2 cups of cold water, 2 cups of boiling water, 3 tablespoons of sugar.

2 Ask a grown-up to boil 2 cups of water on a stove for you.

3 Mix the flour and cold water together in a bowl. Try to smooth out the lumps.

4 Ask the grown-up to help you. Now, pour the flour and water mixture into the boiling water. Stir the mixture until it boils again.

5 Take the pan off the heat. Pour in the three tablespoons of sugar and stir. The mixture will get thick as it cools.

6 Tear up strips of newspaper and dip them into the cooled paste you have just made.

7 Blow up a balloon until it is the size of your head. Tie the end and set it aside.

8 Mark on the balloon with a waterproof marker the size of the mask you want.

9 Take the wet strips out of the paste and lay them inside the marks you made on the balloon. Make sure you overlap the strips and form them into the size and shape you want the mask to be. Mold a nose and other features that you want. Let the mask dry on the balloon.

10 When the mask is dry, pop the balloon. Ask a grown-up to help you cut holes for a ribbon to hold the mask on your face. You will also need holes for your eyes, nose, and mouth.

11 Paint the mask with water-based paint.

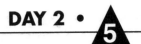

15 Which of the following call for a grown-up's help?

Ⓐ mixing the flour and cold water

Ⓑ blowing up the balloon

Ⓒ boiling the water and cutting the holes

Ⓓ drying the mask

16 How big should the balloon be?

Ⓐ eight inches wide

Ⓑ as big as your head

Ⓒ as big as your hand

Ⓓ as big as you want

17 What fact is most important about letting the paste cool?

Ⓐ It will get thick as it cools.

Ⓑ It is made of flour and water.

Ⓒ It changes color as it cools.

Ⓓ It stays in the same pan you cooked it in.

18 **What is the most likely reason for making the mask on a balloon instead of your face?**

Ⓐ The balloon must be popped to get the mask off.

Ⓑ You don't have to sit with wet newspaper on your face.

Ⓒ You can draw on the balloon with a marker.

Ⓓ You can leave holes for a ribbon on the balloon.

19 **The article says to "mold a nose and other features." The word "features" most likely means**

Ⓐ hair.

Ⓑ glasses.

Ⓒ parts of your face.

Ⓓ arms and legs.

20 **What would happen if you did not overlap the strips of paper on the balloon?**

Ⓐ The mask would blow up.

Ⓑ The mask would have holes in it.

Ⓒ The mask would be scary.

Ⓓ The mask would be too big.

For the open-ended question on the next page, remember to

- Focus your response on the question asked.

- Answer all parts of the question.

- Give a complete explanation.

- Use specific information from the story.

21. Why do you need to pop the balloon when you have completed your work? What would happen if you popped the balloon while the mask is still wet?

_____

_____

_____

_____

_____

_____

_____

_____

_____

_____

_____

_____

_____

_____

_____

STOP

CLOSE YOUR BOOK.

Answer Key
Chapter 1 Answer Explanations

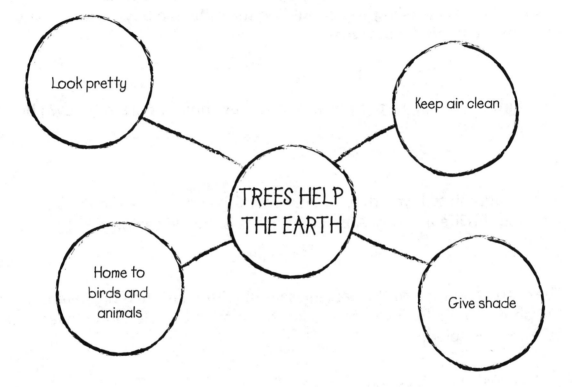

Passage 1: "Little Kittens"

1. **C**

   If you reread the beginning of the poem, you will see that the kittens were fighting over a mouse.

2. **C**

   The woman gets tired of listening to the kittens fight, so she sweeps them outside with a broom.

3. **B**

   The kittens learn to get along. The last two lines of the poem say, "For they found it was better, that stormy night / To lie down and sleep than to quarrel and fight."

Passage 2: "The Man with a Bright Idea: Thomas Edison"

1. A

The passage is a biography. A biography tells about someone's life. The passage begins by telling you about Thomas's life as a boy. Then it tells you some of the things he did when he grew up.

2. C

The third paragraph of this passage says that Thomas started his own business when he was 12.

3. A

This paragraph tells you that Thomas was sick and that he didn't like school. It's about his life as a boy. Answer Choice A is the best answer.

4. D

The sixth paragraph of the passage says that Thomas's first big invention was the phonograph. He invented the lightbulb after this. He didn't invent the telegraph or telephone.

Passage 3: "The Lion and the Mouse"

1. D

Mouse helps Lion at the end of the story. He chews through the net that Lion is trapped in. This sets Lion free.

2. D

In the middle of the story, it says that Crow shouted, "Hunters! We are in great danger! Run away quickly and hide!" So answer choice D is the correct answer.

3. Answers will vary.

Sample answer: The theme of "The Lion and the Mouse" is that anyone can be a good friend. When Mouse is trying to get Lion to set him free in the beginning of the story, Mouse says that he may be able to help Lion some-day. Lion thinks this is very funny. He doesn't see how such a small animal

could ever be able to help him, the King of Beasts. But then Lion gets caught in a net set by hunters. The other animals have left the forest and no one is around to help but Mouse. Mouse chews through the net and Lion goes free.

Chapter 2 Answer Explanations

A pasecki is a hand. The words "raise" and "question" and "call out" offer clues.

Passage 1: "My Shadow"

1. A

The speaker in the poem is saying that the shadow is different from most children because it grows very fast.

2. C

You can find this answer by substituting "a clue" for "a notion." While answer choice A might also seem correct, choice C is a better answer. It's more specific; the shadow hasn't got "a clue" of how children should play.

3. C

You can also find this answer by substituting the answer options for the word "sort." Be careful, however; this doesn't work every time!

Passage 2: Excerpt from *Black Beauty*

1. A

When the mother horse "whinnied" to the younger horse, she calls to the younger horse to come here.

2. C

You can find this answer by looking at the context clues. The mother loved their master; the other horses liked him.

3. C

If you pluck a berry, you pick it. Choice C is the best answer.

Passage 3: "Nature Newsletter"

1. **B**

   An award is a prize. People—or groups—who win a contest usually get an award.

2. **C**

   You can find this answer by crossing out answer options that you know are incorrect. A squirrel can't flap, and it's not bouncing through the air. "Sail" is a better answer than "move," so answer choice C is best.

3. **D**

   When you reuse something, you use it again.

Chapter 3 Answer Explanations

Practice Passage: "The World's Best Banana Milk Shake"

1. **D**

   Read each answer choice carefully. The purpose of Step 1 is not to keep a banana fresh. It also isn't to tell you how to make the milk shake cold. It isn't a summary, either. Answer choice D is the best. Step 1 tells you to peel and freeze the banana.

2. Answers will vary.

   Sample answer: The purpose of the blender is to mix the banana and the milk together.

Passage 1: "How to Fly a Kite"

1. **C**

   If you look at the picture, it is showing you how to hold a kite based on the directions in the passage.

2. **B**

   This answer is right in the passage. The passage says that you should stop letting out string if your kite starts to go down.

3. Answers will vary.

Sample answer: To land a kite, you should start winding up the string slowly. This will make the kite come in closer to you. Once the kite gets close enough that you can reach it, you can grab it and pull it in.

Passage 2: "How to Make a Sock Puppet"

1. A

In Step 4, it says that cloth is used to make the puppet's mouth.

2. A

Step 8 of the passage tells you to cut out two one-inch circles for the eyes.

3. D

Step 9 tells you to add small triangles along your sock puppet's back to make it look like a dragon.

Passage 3: "How to Have Your Own Treasure Hunt"

1. A

The purpose of Step 2 is to tell you what you need to have a treasure hunt. The phrase "Gather your supplies" should give you a clue.

2. D

The picture with Step 1 is just emphasizing that you should call your friends to invite them to the treasure hunt.

3. Answers will vary.

Sample answer: Your opening clue should be just a few sentences that will help your friends find their treasure. It could rhyme or be like a riddle, but it doesn't have to. Your opening clue will lead your readers to the next clue.

4. Answers will vary.

Sample answer: The passage says that you should pick a good hiding place for your starting point. You shouldn't pick a place that's very easy, but it shouldn't be too hard, either. You don't want to pick a place that your friend will never find.

Chapter 4 Answer Explanations

Author's Purpose

1. To convince

2. To entertain

3. To inform

4. To teach

5. To describe

6. To teach

Prediction

Answers will vary. Students may say that something shocking or scary will happen, like the front door will swing open.

Passage 1: "Sweet Treat"

1. **A**

    The author of this passage writes about sweet potatoes. The author tells how you can make them and where you can buy them.

2. **A**

    In the beginning of the passage, the author says that sweet potatoes contain vitamins and minerals, so the author thinks that sweet potatoes are good for you.

3. Answers will vary.

    Sample answer: At the end of the passage, it says to add brown sugar to make sweet potatoes sweet. If you add a lot of brown sugar, your sweet potatoes will be very, very sweet.

Passage 2: Excerpt from *The Jungle Book*

1. Answers will vary.

    Sample answer: The father says that the mongoose will come in and out of the house all day as long as Timmy does not pick it up by the tail. This leads the reader to believe that the mongoose wouldn't come in the house if Timmy picks it up by the tail.

2. **C**

    The author wrote this story to entertain. The author is telling a story about a mongoose, so answer choice C is best. You can tell that the story is make-believe because the mongoose speaks at the end of the story.

3. Answer will vary.

    Sample answer: The mongoose might get into trouble because he says that he plans to find out things about the house. He also might do something to help the people, because they saved his life and he seems to like them.

Passage 3: "Rooms of Water"

1. **C**

    The author wrote this passage to tell readers all about a great aquarium. While answer choice A might also seem correct, the author only suggests that readers go to the aquarium. The author doesn't try to tell readers how to get there.

2. **D**

    Animals in the Meet-a-Creature room are small and get held, so this is the best answer.

3. Answers will vary.

    Sample answer: If I went to the aquarium, I would definitely look at the big tanks first. I think big fish—even sharks—are amazing. This is what I would most like to see.

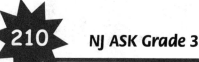

Chapter 5 Answer Explanations

Practice Passage: "Time with Dad"

3.   Answers will vary.

Sample answer: I would like to do the things that Greta and her dad do. I like to help my parents cook—and I love to eat spaghetti. I also enjoy going on long walks with family and friends. And I think learning how to use a hammer and nail would be really fun.

Passage 1: "Autumn's Amazing Leaves"

1.   **C**

Leaves in autumn turn bright, pretty colors. Most people look forward to this time of year and think that the leaves are very beautiful.

2.   **A**

The third paragraph of the article explains that the leaves change color in the fall because there is less sunlight. This causes the chlorophyll to break down. In places where it is warmer, the sun shines all through the year, so the leaves stay green.

3.   Answers will vary.

Sample answer: I think the leaves in autumn are very beautiful. They turn the mountains bright colors. It looks as if an artist painted the countryside. As the article says, I look forward to this time when the chlorophyll breaks down and the leaves change colors. Also, as the article says, I wish it would last longer!

Passage 2: "The Best Game in the World"

1.   **C**

The second paragraph explains that the object of the game is to own more than everyone else—to own everything if you can. So you could win the game by owning a lot of houses and hotels.

2. A

The end of the article says that the game hasn't changed much over the years and that most versions of the game played in the United States have Atlantic City street names.

3. Answers will vary.

Sample answer: I do play Monopoly with my family and friends. I really enjoy the game. I like to try to own as much property as I can. I also like to be the banker, the person who holds the money. As the article says, most of the games today have Atlantic City street names, even though some of these places don't exist anymore. I like this. I know the places on the game board very well.

Passage 3: "Beatrix Potter"

1. A

You can tell from the article that Beatrix liked children. She wrote her books for children. When she married, she and her husband kept animals on their farm for children to see.

2. Answers will vary.

Sample answer: When Beatrix and her brother were young, they spent hours in the woods trying to learn all they could about different kinds of animals. Then they kept many different kinds of animals as pets. Beatrix had a hedgehog named Mrs. Tiggy-winkle and a pig named Pig-Wig! Some of these animals later appeared in Beatrix's stories.

3. Answers will vary.

Sample answer: I think I would definitely like to read Beatrix's books. Like Beatrix, I like animals, especially funny ones like hedgehogs and pigs. The story says that children all over England loved her story *The Tale of Peter Rabbit*. I think that I would like it too.

Chapter 6 Answer Explanations

Characters

The two characters in "Learning to Fly" are Little Robin and Mother Robin.

Special Language and Type

1. The author put the word "AGAIN" in capital letters to show that the bike chain has fallen off many times before.

2. Lilly calls her bike "my friend" because her bike is like a friend who has let her down.

Passage 1: "Ali's Kitten"

1. **A**

   The story is about a kitten. But the main character is Ali. Ali is the one who says and does the most in the story.

2. **C**

   The first paragraph of the story tells you that Ali is lying in the sun, but it is getting colder and she wonders what she and Nan will do all day during the winter.

3. **C**

   The story says that winter is coming, but it's still warm. The story takes place in the fall.

Passage 2: "When I Grow Up"

1. **B**

   Most of this story takes place in the third-grade classroom. This is the setting of the story.

2. **B**

   Kyle is the main character in the story, because he says and does the most. He is also the character with a problem.

3. **C**

   Kyle's problem is that he does not know what he wants to be when he grows up, so he can't write his essay for Parents' Night.

4. Answers will vary.

   Sample answer: Kyle solves his problem by talking to Mrs. Dixon. She asks him what he likes to do and where he likes to spend his time. She thinks that he might like to work as a librarian—and she is right. Once he knows this, Kyle can write his essay.

Passage 3: "The Emperor and Nightingale"

1. **A**

   The end of the story takes place in the emperor's bedroom, but most of the story takes place in the palace.

2. **D**

   The real nightingale is not beautiful, but he sings beautifully.

3. **C**

   The exclamation shows that the pop was loud and probably startled people.

4. **C**

   The end of the story takes place in the emperor's bedroom. He is in bed, because he is ill.

Practice Test 1 Answer Explanations

Writing Task 1

Sample answer: A group of Native American families is going on a journey to find a new village. They had to leave their old village when settlers came and made them leave. They were able to collect some of their things before they had to get away from the settlers, and now they are walking through the woods to find a new home. Another group of adults and children is following this group. The grown-ups put on happy faces so that their children won't be scared. The boys are too young to understand what has happened, and so they run around and play games while they travel. They will soon find a new place to live, far away from the settlers, and they will start building a new village.

"A Trip of Tests"

1. **B**   W3   Extrapolation of Information

   The special day discussed in the story is the day that the Lenape go to visit their neighbors on the other side of the forest.

2. **D**   W1   Theme

   In the story, someone from every family offers something that helps the group get to their neighbors' village.

3. **B**   W2   Supporting Detail

   Mitsin's father is able to lead the group in the right direction by following the rising sun. While the other answer choices include details in the story, they do not explain how Mitsin's father helped the group.

4. **C**   W3   Extrapolation of Information

   When Wisawe's mother scares away the bear, Seke thinks that she is brave and wishes that his parents were brave enough to scare away a bear.

5. **D**   W3   Extrapolation of Information

   Seke's parents build the canoe so that the group can get across the large creek to their neighbors' village. Though they do end up showing that they are useful, too, this is not why they decided to build the canoe.

6. **A** A4 Drawing Conclusions

Seke learns that his parents are brave and smart like the other parents in the group. Answer choice B is not true, because there is nothing in the story that proves they can't scare away a bear. Answer choice C is not correct, because the narrator does not state that they don't know how to swim across; the narrator states that not even the strongest swimmers would be able to swim across. Nothing in the story suggests that they are the greatest parents in the village, so answer choice D is also incorrect.

7. **A3** Forming of Opinions

Sample answer: The first parent to help the group is Wisawe's mother. She bravely saves their food from a very large bear by clapping her hands and yelling to scare it away. When the group gets lost, Mitsin's father figures out which direction is the right one by looking at the sun. Then, when the group comes to a big creek that looks impossible to cross, they think they will have to turn around and go back home, but Seke's parents get the idea to make a canoe. No one thinks that it will work, but Seke's parents make the tools that they need to make a canoe. Then they make a canoe large enough to carry the entire group across the creek to the neighbors' village. They save the trip by getting them to where they wanted to go.

I don't think that any parent was more helpful or did anything more important than the other parents. Seke's parents finally got them across the creek and to the village, but they would not have reached the creek at all if Wisawe's mother and Mitsin's father had not helped also. Maybe Seke's parents were most helpful only because they taught their son an important lesson.

"Down the Drain"

8. **A** W4 Supporting Detail

Of the events in the choices, the first to happen is when Jason stops on his way home from school. All the other events happen later in the story.

9. **A** W4 Supporting Detail

Jason hears a strange cheeping noise coming from the drain. None of the other choices fits the details in the story.

10. B   A4   Drawing Conclusions

The only choice that fits the story's details is B. Babies are not very old compared to their mother.

11. B   W3   Extrapolation of Information

At one point, Mrs. Uchida says, "Well, fire fighters rescue cats from trees all the time." The other answers are not facts from the story.

12. D   A3   Forming of Opinions

All the characters care about what happens to the baby ducks. The other answer choices are opinions that not all of the characters share.

13. B   A4   Making Judgments, Drawing Conclusions

If everyone started saying what to do, it would take much longer to get the job done. Also, if the firefighters became confused, there is more of a chance that someone would get hurt.

14.   W3   Extrapolation of Information

Sample answer: The mother duck was afraid that the children would hurt her babies so she tried to chase them away. Hanson put the babies over in the park so that the mother duck could safely collect them and take them away with her.

Writing Task 2

Sample answer: I like to use my imagination to pretend that I am a dinosaur hunter. My sister pretends with me. We walk around in the woods behind our house and use a magnifying glass to look for clues on the ground. We wear big hats so flying dinosaurs will not be able to attack our heads. We make dinosaur tracks in the dirt and then pretend to find them. We pretend that trees are dinosaurs and that they are chasing us, so we have to run away from them. We carry big sticks and swing them at pretend dinosaurs to scare them. We have a lot of fun pretending that we are dinosaur hunters. This is one of the reasons that using our imagination is valuable. It is also good because it keeps us busy so we don't feel bored, and it lets us travel to times and places in our minds that we would never be able to go to in real life.

"Chickasaw Day Camp"

15. D   W4   Paraphrasing, Vocabulary

The purpose of learning something is to help you get better at it. Students should be able to tell that "improve" means "get better" from the clues in the passage, such as the word "class" and the questions that are asked before the word appears in the passage.

16. C   W2   Supporting Detail

The passage states that swimming lessons and free swims can be taken at all times throughout the day because the camp has four pools.

17. A   W5   Text Organization

The first paragraph introduces reasons why Camp Chickasaw is a great way for kids to spend their summer. The list of activities that children can participate in at the camp comes after the introduction (answer choice B). The passage does not explain why children go to different camps for special interests (answer choice C), nor does it explain how parents can find out more about different camps (answer choice D).

18. C   A4   Drawing Conclusions

The passage mentions calling the camp before signing up for music lessons after it talks about the fact that some instruments are available at the camp and some must be brought from home. Parents should call to find out what instruments are at the camp and then figure out whether their child needs to bring an instrument from home.

19. A   W4   Paraphrasing/Vocabulary

Group leaders are in charge of a group of 15 campers. Leaders are not there to look at (answer choice B) campers, order them around (answer choice C), or act like campers (answer choice D).

20. B   A4   Drawing Conclusions

Three of the activities listed require children to be active. One activity, computers, does not require children to run around. If a child is tired, this might be the best activity for that child.

21. A3 Forming of Opinions

Sample answer: Children need different clothing on different days, depending on the kinds of activities they will do that day. Some clothing may not be comfortable enough for some activities. Some clothing might get ruined when kids do certain things. For example, a child who was painting that day might want to wear an old shirt so he or she wouldn't have to worry about getting paint on a nice shirt. A kid who was taking dance on a certain day would have to wear clothes that were comfortable and let the kid move around a lot. A child who was taking computers one day might not need to worry about wearing comfortable or older clothes, depending on what else the child was signed up for that day. The different clothing lets kids be comfortable, and it keeps parents from worrying that their child might ruin his or her nice clothing.

Practice Test 2 Answer Explanations

Writing Task 1

Sample answer: Two sisters, Kate and Melissa, are upset because their cat, Whiskers, is missing. Whiskers doesn't go outside, but Kate thinks that he may have gotten out by accident. Kate and Melissa look for Whiskers in their neighborhood, but they can't find him. As time passes, they become even more worried. Finally, they spot Whiskers under a bush in their neighbor's yard. He runs out from under the bush and jumps into Kate's arms. Kate hugs him. Kate and Melissa are very happy. They take Whiskers back home with them.

"Important Promises"

1. **C W3** Extrapolation of Information

    In the beginning of the story, Galen promises to clean her room but then decides that it is too nice to stay inside. She rides her bike instead.

2. **C W4** Paraphrasing/Retelling

    When the author says that Galen is ashamed, it means that Galen is sorry she did not keep her promises.

3. C   W3   Extrapolation of Information

The main lesson that Galen learns is that it is important to keep your promises—to do what you say that you are going to do. While the other answer choices tell about important things too, they do not state the main lesson that Galen learns.

4. A   W5   Text Organization

At the end of this story, Galen talks to her parents in her bedroom. She is very tired and wants to sleep.

5. C   W1   Theme

The theme is the message the author is trying to get across. The message in this story is about promises. Both answer choices B and C mention promises, but the message is not that you should stop making promises. It is that you should keep them.

6. B   W5   Text Organization

In the last paragraph, Galen tells her parents that she understands the importance of a promise. The author included this paragraph to show that Galen has learned an important lesson about promises.

7. A3   Forming of Opinions

Sample answer: Galen makes promises to her parents, her friend Patty, and to her sister, Beatrice. She promises her parents that she will clean her room. She promises Patty that she will help her find Mr. Stripes, her cat. And she promises Beatrice that she will help her with her math homework.

All of these promises are important, but I think the most important promise Galen made was to Patty. Patty is really worried about her cat, and her cat might be lost or in danger. Galen should have helped Patty right away.

Writing Task 2

Sample answer: When summer first started, I had no idea of the adventure I would have. My uncle called and asked if I would like to go up in a rocket to visit the planet Mars. I yelled, "Yes!" My mom and dad helped me to get ready. Soon we were on our way to Cape Kennedy.

As we flew through space I saw shooting stars and other planets. Sometimes I got to float around in the cabin. We landed on Mars and visited my cousins who live there now. We had great fun roaming the planet in our spacesuits.

When we came back home I told all of my friends about the trip. We all planned to go into space together when we grow up. We want to find other new and exciting places.

"How to Grow Sunflowers"

8. B   W5   Text Organization

The first paragraph discusses what sunflowers look like and tells the reader that sunflower seeds are good to eat. It's an introduction.

9. B   W3   Extrapolation of Information

The article says that you can use a stick to stake the sunflower. This means that you tie the sunflower to the stick with string to keep it from bending and breaking.

10. D   W3   Extrapolation of Information

The author says that you should mix the peat into the dirt before you plant the seeds. The peat helps the soil become good for growing.

11. C   W4   Paraphrasing/Retelling

"Soaked" means "very wet." The word "wet" in the sentence gives a clue.

12. A W4 Paraphrasing/Retelling

When you harvest the seeds, you take them out of the sunflower. Answer choice A, "gather," is the best answer.

13. A W5 Text Organization

This article gives instruction. It teaches you how to grow sunflowers. Answer choice A is the best answer.

14. A4 Drawing Conclusions

Sample answer: When you thin out sunflower seeds, you pull out the smaller plants so that the larger plants are farther apart. You do this because the larger plants are usually the healthy, strong ones. Thinning out the smaller plants gives the larger plants more room to grow.

"Make a Papier-Mâché Mask"

15. C W3 Extrapolation of Information

The steps that call for adult help are boiling water on a stove and cutting holes in the mask. Answer choice (C) is correct. Adult help is not needed to mix the flour and water (A), blow up the balloon (B), or dry the mask (D).

16. B W4 Paraphrasing/Retelling

Step 6 says to "blow up a balloon until it is the size of your head." Answer choice (B) is the only correct answer.

17. A W5 Recognition of Supporting Details

Step 5 says that the mixture will get thick as it cools, which is the most important fact about the paste. Answer choice (A) is correct. Answer (B) is a fact, but it is not important about the paste cooling. Answer (C) is not a fact from the list. Answer (D) is not important.

18. B W5 Recognition of Supporting Details

It would be uncomfortable to have wet newspaper on your face, so (B) is the correct answer. You could peel the mask off your face, so (A) is incorrect. You could make marks on your face, so (C) is incorrect. The holes go in the mask, so (D) is incorrect.

19. C W4   Paraphrasing/Retelling

Since a nose is a part of a face, (C) is the correct answer. The other answers do not have the same meaning as "features."

20. B A4   Drawing Conclusions

The directions say to overlap the strips of paper. Thinking it through you can understand that any spaces left without a covering would become a hole when the balloon is popped.

21. B W3   Extrapolation of Information

Sample answer: You need to pop the balloon when you are finished so that you can put the mask on your face. You can't use the mask if the balloon is in the way. If you popped the balloon before the mask dried then the mask would fall apart.